The
H.P. LOVECRAFT
Companion

Philip A. Shreffler

The
H.P. LOVECRAFT
Companion

GREENWOOD PRESS
WESTPORT, CONNECTICUT • LONDON, ENGLAND

Library of Congress Cataloging in Publication Data

Shreffler, Philip A
    The H. P. Lovecraft companion.

    Bibliography: p.
    Includes index.
    1. Lovecraft, Howard Phillips, 1890-1937—Criticism
and interpretation. I. Title.
PS3523.0833Z86   813'.5'2   76-52605
ISBN 0-8371-9482-2

Library of Congress Catalog Card Number: 76-52605
ISBN: 0-8371-9482-2

First published in 1977

Greenwood Press, Inc.
51 Riverside Avenue, Westport, Connecticut 06880

Printed in the United States of America

10 9 8 7 6 5 4 3 2

TO CHRISTY

Contents

Illustrations

Preface

Like his hero Edgar Allan Poe, Howard Phillips Lovecraft, the reclusive author of horror stories from Providence, Rhode Island, never achieved during his own lifetime the kind of fame he deserved. Lovecraft's fiction was known primarily to the readers of a pulp magazine called *Weird Tales*, which began publication in 1923. By the time of his death in 1937, Lovecraft had seen no major, book-length collection of his stories. It was not until 1939 that a small publishing enterprise known as Arkham House brought out the first Lovecraft book — *The Outsider*. And it took over twenty years more for publishers to see the financial advantage in issuing numerous inexpensive, soft-bound mass-market editions of Lovecraft's tales of terror.

Of course, all along there had been a corps of readers dedicated to the genre of weird fiction who knew Lovecraft to be its twentieth-century master. These individuals went on quietly reading and admiring Lovecraft, communicating among themselves and congregating inobtrusively in the flickering shadows of Lovecraft's literary light.

In the meantime, with the advent of the age of Sputnik, popular interest in the supernatural horror story seemed to wane, being replaced by science fiction tales that had a sound basis in factual possibility. Ghosts seemed to give way to rocket ships, witchcraft and sorcery to time travel and alien civilizations.

Yet the undercurrent of fascination with fantasy and horror continued to exist, and it was possibly due to the widespread disillusionment with the ravages of modern technology that a great revival of interest in fantastic worlds began to occur in the 1960s. J. R. R. Tolkein's hobbit novels took the college compuses by storm, and sales of books by A. Conan Doyle and Edgar Rice Burroughs soared. And, not remarkably, over a million paperback copies of H. P. Lovecraft's works were sold between 1970 and 1973 alone.

Perhaps one of the greatest moments in the history of Lovecraftian letters occurred on Hallowe'en of 1975 when two dozen horror and fantasy writers and 500 Lovecraft devotees gathered in Providence for the First Annual World Fantasy Convention—a convocation dedicated, that year, wholly to Lovecraft. Tours of the Providence that Lovecraft had immortalized in his fiction were organized, writers who had known him delivered eulogies, readings from his stories were given, and the first H. P. Lovecraft awards for excellence in fantastic fiction were presented. The mayor of Providence made an appearance, gratifying the assemblage with the news that he was planning to place a statue of the master on Lovecraft's beloved College Hill near the Brown University campus.

Wandering among the loyal who had attended the Lovecraft convention was like stepping into a dreamland. Everywhere one turned, it seemed, there were small groups of people discussing the *Necronomicon*, a fictional magical incantation book invented by Lovecraft. There was even a contingent of students wearing red shirts bearing the words "Miskatonic University"—the fictional institution of higher learning, housing a copy of the fictional *Necronomicon*, that Lovecraft had placed in the fictional town of Arkham, Massachusetts.

I think that moment revealed to me as clearly as anything ever had how very real the literary world of H. P. Lovecraft had become, with its transdimensional demons, cowled sorcerers, and mountaintop gods.

I sneaked off into Lovecraft's world as a boy. I had, and fortunately still have, a paperback book called *The Macabre Reader* that contains HPL's "The Thing on the Doorstep." When the Lovecraft stories came out in paperback editions in the 1960s, vague and wonderfully horrible memories slowly shambled back into my mind—memories of the boy I was, frightened and alarmed by things that H. P. Lovecraft had set into sinister motion and that had been a part of my subconscious ever since.

Even by the time I had been through college and graduate school, I had not forgotten my boyhood friends—the monsters of dreamland. In fact, I learned that I could rarely pick up a work of American literature without finding it fairly teeming with monsters. Monsters, I found, were simply a part of the American consciousness, from the Puritan devils of Cotton Mather to the backwoods bogeymen of Mark Twain.

It was this discovery, as much as anything else, that inclined me to put together a book on H. P. Lovecraft. For Lovecraft, I knew, had constructed a fantastic and horrific cosmos as complete as those of Hawthorne and Poe. Lovecraft could, to quote Hawthorne, "dream strange things and make them look like truth."

In this book I am not trying to throw much light on the literary dream-scape of H. P. Lovecraft. After all, light only destroys monsters and too many of them have expired from sheer exhaustion in this technological age. Instead, I hope what I have done is to offer a roadmap through Lovecraft's nightmare and to provide a guidebook for explorers of his archaic, crumbling universe of horror.

—P. A. S.

Acknowledgments

I wish to express my grateful appreciation to the following individuals and institutions for their valuable help in the preparation of this book:

Forrest D. Hartmann, of Arkham House Publishers, Sauk City, Wisconsin, for permission to quote from the works of H. P. Lovecraft and for permission to reproduce Lovecraft's map of Arkham.

Donald Cochran for permission to reproduce his map of Lovecraft's Dreamland.

Rachell Rosenblum for her pen-and-ink illustrations and rendering of maps.

John Symonds, representing the estate of Aleister Crowley, for permission to quote ten lines from Crowley's "Hymn to Pan."

Robert Howie, historian of St. Michael's Church, Marblehead, Massachusetts, for contributing information on St. Michael's.

Barton L. St. Armand, Dirk Mosig, R. Alain Everts, David E. Schultz, Thomas Collins, and the numerous other Lovecraft scholars who gave of their time in providing aid in this project.

John Bennett Shaw, who provided a starting point.

Barry Hapner, Eric Otten, and Nils Hardin, who aided in bibliographical research.

The Essex Institute of Salem, Massachusetts, the Newburyport, Massachusetts Historical Society and the staff of the Wilbraham,

Massachusetts Public Library for their help with historical data.

And my wife, Christy Beckmann Shreffler, for her useful suggestions and encouragement all along the way.

The
H.P. LOVECRAFT
Companion

There have been few writers, if any, who have had as much impact on the twentieth-century supernatural horror story as H. P. Lovecraft (1890-1937), the dark dreamer of Providence, Rhode Island. During a professional writing career that spanned sixteen of his forty-seven years, Lovecraft's name became virtually synonymous with the weird tale, and it remains so to such a great degree that his work is not only enjoying a great recrudescence today but is still being widely imitated in pastiche and has become the topic of scholarly investigation in both the United States and Europe.

It is really not too surprising that this should be the case, because Lovecraft's fiction deals with one of man's most elementary emotions: fear. As Lovecraft noted in the introduction to "Supernatural Horror in Literature": "The oldest and strongest emotion of mankind is fear, and the oldest and strongest kind of fear is fear of the unknown." There are two key terms in this seemingly obvious statement that are of paramount importance in Lovecraft's work. The first of course is "fear," for this is primarily what his horror stories concern themselves with. The second, and more subtle, concept is that of "the oldest and strongest emotion of mankind."

Although he dealt with these primitive emotions, to say that Love-

1 Lovecraft's literary theory

craft would have subscribed to the scientific mysticism of C. G. Jung and to the formalized theory of the racial unconscious is probably in error. Lovecraft was a fairly hard-boiled scientific materialist who tended not to believe in what could not be measured or perceived sensorily. But, at the same time, he had a deep sensitivity to the horrific qualities of antiquity, an understanding that the further back into history he could trace the patterns of human belief and behavior, the further he could remove his fiction from the known. And in approaching the antique unknown, he felt, the easier it is to stimulate fear.

This is why so many of Lovecraft's tales root themselves in a mythos of unseen and undimensioned monsters that existed before the advent of man on earth, or else involve fantasy lands that are at once strange and familiar, often having derivative place names, like Sarnath, which is an archeological site in India. Prehistory, Lovecraft's theory might state, equals the unknown, and the unknown yields fear.

In this way the scope of Lovecraft's horror stories becomes cosmic in nature; vast sweeps of space and time are the rule rather than the exception. And this is what gives Lovecraft such a peculiarly American character. From the days when English Anglicans hacked Jamestown out of the Virginia swamps and the Puritan Separatists braved the hostile environment of eastern Massachusetts on through to the present time, American writers have responded one way or another to the sheer immensity of their national landscape. What Daniel Boone used to refer to as "elbow room" has been transmuted in the hands of our artists into a kind of huge blank canvas on which grandiose philosophical ideas can be painted on a cosmic scale.

Whereas most European writers and artists, more secure in their sense of place and the tradition of physically settled civilization, have generally focused their art on smaller-scale human occurrences (and here we may except the German Romantics), American artists from the Puritans, the Romantics, the naturalists, and through to the present century have dealt chiefly with the most massive and perplexing problems of philosophy: the nature of being, the validity of knowledge, questions of universal morality and aesthetics.

Lovecraft, too, addressed himself to some of these same issues. Ontology and epistemology both play a role in stories like "Celephais" and "Through the Gates of the Silver Key"; moral allegory is the primary function of "The Street" and "The White Ship"; and the aesthetic question becomes the focal point of "The Unnamable" and "The Hound."

But confronting these philosophical questions in the way that a Hawthorne or a Melville would was not Lovecraft's main intent. If he could touch on them along the way, that was clear profit. The major impetus behind Lovecraft's fiction, however, was purely to frighten, to excite and elevate the sensibilities of the reader in such a way that he could experience not merely shock but horror on a cosmic level.

In this regard, Lovecraft most closely resembles Poe — "my God of Fiction," Lovecraft admitted. Many critics may dispute the popularly held thesis that Lovecraft's fiction measures up to that of Poe. The fact remains, however, that Lovecraft did carefully mold his literary theory on Poe's (a fuller discussion of which appears later in this chapter) and that Lovecraft's literary value has been championed recently primarily by French academics like Maurice Lévy of the University of Toulouse and in the pages of the French literary magazine *L'Herne*, just as the standard of Poe was taken up by Baudelaire in the nineteenth century. It is also worthy of note that the first doctoral dissertation on Lovecraft appeared in Italy and that his works have been translated into many foreign languages, including German and Japanese.

Yet European recognition does not alter the fact that Poe sought to express "the grim phantasm FEAR" in a way that was universal among men and cosmically "out of Time and out of Space." And Lovecraft's similar recognition does not alter this American quality in his work.

At the same time, it is untrue to say that Lovecraft's fiction is informed wholly by American literature. Indeed, in his long essay survey of horrific fiction, "Supernatural Horror in Literature," Lovecraft cites as many British works as American ones as having a central influence on the genre of the weird tale. And there can be no mistake, as students of Lovecraft's work discover, about its being touched with the technical characteristics of the British horror story.

"Supernatural Horror in Literature" traces the major appearances of straight horror stories and literary works with elements of horror in them, from ancient times to Lovecraft's own present and shows Lovecraft's knowledge of the history of the weird tale to be encyclopedic. There are two especially instructive aspects of this essay. First, we may see which literary works Lovecraft held to be important and therefore suspect that these works affected his writing in some sense.

Second, and more important, the essay permits us a glimpse at the depth and breadth of Lovecraft's own literary knowledge as well as the quality of his understanding of literature. And that knowledge and understanding are, for the most part, impressive.

The essay begins with mention of the *Book of Enoch* and the *Claviculae of Solomon* (sometimes called the *Keys of Solomon*), two ancient Semitic grimoires, or occult instruction books on ceremonial magic. In a scant two pages following this, Lovecraft goes on to discuss briefly "Druidic, Graeco-Roman and Christian faiths" associated with the secret fertility cults of agricultural societies, Teutonic mythology, *Walpurgisnacht* and Hallowe'en, the Black Mass, and a few famous occultists. All of this suggests a sound knowledge of the various manifestations of occultism throughout history, as well as Lovecraft's own familiarity with the textual material pertaining to it, including Sir James Frazer's outstanding summary of fertility cults, *The Golden Bough*, published only four years before Lovecraft undertook his essay. The essay also treats the major periods of gothicism as well as the history of the horror story in Continental Europe, Great Britain, and America.

But the primary influences on his fiction were derived from nineteenth- and twentieth-century England and America. From England Lovecraft seems to have gained his expertise in technical craftsmanship; the philosophical portion of his literary theory was nurtured in the intellectual soil of America.

LOVECRAFT AND THE BRITISH HORROR STORY

It is very difficult to pinpoint all of the literary influences on an author's writing, not only for the critical student but often for the author himself. Fortunately, however, "Supernatural Horror in Literature" provides some clues. And they are only clues, because nowhere in the essay does Lovecraft state whether or not a given horror story writer impressed himself upon Lovecraft's own fiction.

Yet there are at least two ways of proceeding with this investigation: (1) we may compare and contrast the work of other writers to Lovecraft's own, and (2) we may observe which writers Lovecraft treats in the greatest depth and to which he devotes the most space.

It is interesting to note that for all the gothic conventions in Lovecraft's fiction—broken-down castles, ruined villages, and the occasional subtly suggested themes of ghosts and vampires—Lovecraft himself seems to have considered the gothic mode something of a passé genre. This is true to such an extent that in "Supernatural Horror in Literature" Lovecraft devotes three sections to the gothic tradition and establishes "The Weird Tradition in the British Isles" as another section, separated from his discussion of gothicism by an examination of "The Weird Tradition in America."

Lovecraft has only faint praise for the gothicists, apparently seeing them as initiators of the modern weird tale rather than horrific fiction's mainstay. In effect, Lovecraft found gothicism too cliché ridden, too formulaic, and too conventional to achieve true weirdness.

In sketching out the weird tradition of a number of classical writers, through the ballad-tales of the Middle Ages and into the Gothic period, Lovecraft touches lightly on some of the greatest works of literature—among them *Beowulf, Morte d'Arthur, Macbeth*, and Goethe's *Faust*—and deliberately considers each of them only as it relates to the supernatural motif. But it is when he comes to discuss Walpole's *Castle of Otranto* that he makes an important statement about his understanding of what weird fiction must do. He says of *Otranto*: "The story—tedious, artificial and melodramatic—is further impaired by a brisk and prosaic style whose urbane sprightliness nowhere permits the creation of a truly weird atmosphere."

By today's standards, all fiction, including horror stories, must be written in a slick, brisk, and sprightly style or it is likely to discourage at least the casual reader. Lovecraft's indictment of *The Castle Of Otranto* for that reason sounds archaic and pedantic, almost like the rhetoric of a dilettante critic. But the fact is that Lovecraft is being perfectly consistent with a literary theory in which he not only believed but that he had also seen used successfully in the best supernatural fiction, notably in the works of his hero Edgar Allan Poe, about whom he wrote later in the essay.

Two other Gothic writers considered to be of importance were Ann Radcliffe and Matthew Gregory Lewis, whose enormously popular works firmly established the Gothic tradition in Europe. It was also Radcliffe, Lovecraft maintains, who influenced the early American novelist Charles Brockden Brown, author of the dark and melancholy *Arthur Mervyn* and *Wieland*.

Seeing gothicism progressing through three stages, from the mid-eighteenth century to the turn of the twentieth century, Lovecraft identifies numerous works that highlight the genre. Among these, in addition to Walpole's *Castle of Otranto*, Radcliffe's *Mysteries of*

Udolpho, and Lewis's *The Monk*, are Charles Robert Maturin's *Melmoth, the Wanderer*, William Beckford's *History of the Caliph of Vathek*, and Mary Shelley's *Frankenstein*.

In times closer to Lovecraft's own, the stories of Edward Bulwer-Lytton are singled out, as are the works of J. Sheridan LeFanu, Wilkie Collins, H. Rider Haggard, Sir Arthur Conan Doyle, H. G. Wells, and Robert Louis Stevenson. However, of this latter impressive listing, only Bulwer-Lytton is discussed in any detail.

The simple fact would appear to be that although Lovecraft recognized these works as substantial contributions to the field of weird fiction, he did not consider them seminal enough to his own way of thinking about the genre to digress at length about any of them. But when Lovecraft reaches "The Weird Tradition in the British Isles," he becomes excited about several English authors, devoting a great deal of space to them. And it is in this section also that we begin to encounter a series of literary works that plainly had a substantial influence on Lovecraft's own style. We can find in Lovecraft's plots some recognizable motifs and patterns from these works.

Probably the two most famous works to come from the period mentioned by Lovecraft are Oscar Wilde's *The Picture of Dorian Gray* and Bram Stoker's *Dracula*. In Wilde's novel it is a supernatural event that occasions the visible manifestation of a man's own internal folly and evil. The idea of making moral corruption physically sensible seems to have been almost a staple plot idea for turn-of-the-century British authors of weird fiction. It is Stevenson's main theme in *The Strange Case of Dr. Jekyll and Mr. Hyde*, and Arthur Machen employs it in *The Novel of the White Powder*, wherein a drug causes the evil in one of the story's characters to exhibit itself so explicitly as to reduce him to a bubbling, fetid pool of slime. This theme occurs in Lovecraft as well, particularly in the terrible demise of Wilbur Whateley in "The Dunwich Horror" as well as in the narrator's regression to the primitive state of his ancestors in "The Rats in the Walls."

Lovecraft considered Stoker's *Dracula* to be "a tale now justly assigned a permanent place in English letters." Yet Lovecraft also points out that *Dracula* was so successful a work of its kind that it touched off a series of imitations. While Lovecraft himself had no apparent objections to incorporating into his own work the basic themes that had appeared in other horror stories, he was clearly not interested in blatant imitation, with the major exception of his Lord Dunsany imitations. This may be why he never wrote a straightforward vampire story but at the same time did not shy away from vampiric suggestion in tales like "The Shunned House" and "The Case of Charles Dexter Ward."

If one characteristic separates Lovecraft from much of the weird tradition in Great Britain, it is that the British horror story concentrates so frequently on a localized supernatural event or series of events. More often than not, it seems, the English wrote conventional ghost or haunted-house stories in which there is a single supernatural entity that haunts a limited spatial area. As we have already noted, however, Lovecraft's supernatural beings reach out across time and space, and the purview of their influence is often not only worldwide but truly universal.

With this in mind, it is more understandable that Lovecraft should have been drawn to writers like M. P. Shiel, Walter de la Mare, Arthur Machen, M. R. James, and Lord Dunsany. In the best works of these writers, and particularly in that of Machen, the thematic focus is pervasive cosmic evil that lurks just behind visible reality and always threatens to burst forth into the prosaic, mundane world. These are not the tales of unruly spirits or of ghosts that wander around castles looking for their heads; they are not stories for telling in the crackling warmth of a Christmas Eve fire. Rather, they are tales of human beings caught in a web of destructive forces—forces that the authors may only dimly hint at and that are never fully understood by those involved with them.

It is important to note here that the cosmicism—the universal scale—characterizing American literature and the work of H. P. Lovecraft seems to appear also in the works of these few British writers. Yet there is a difference in American cosmicism and the similar British response. The American propensity to deal with human life and thought on this large scale grew as a result of the size of the unsettled American continent. In its early days America was a land of almost infinite possibility; it was an enormous blank slate on which new ideas might be written, a place in which Salem witches and white whales might well be conceived of as realities. Britain, on the other hand, was an ancient and settled land, with roots that reached back to the Romans, the Celts, and beyond.

Thus while American cosmicism was derived from spatial latitude, Britain depended on its own antiquity to gain the same literary sense. But because Britain was more secure than America in terms of its sense of place in the spatial and temporal scheme of things, British cosmicism is a far rarer phenomenon than American cosmicism. The cosmic scale in the literature of Britain tended to occur only in the hands of those who were touched personally by a sense of the British mythic heritage. And this inclination would certainly include Arthur Machen, the Welsh mystic who was so deeply interested in Celtic mythology and in the symbol systems of ceremonial magic. Let us state this rather complicated thesis in simpler terms: The cosmic scale of American literature comes from America's vast geography, whereas the cosmic scale in British literature, when present at all, comes from Britain's long history.

In terms of his literary intentions, then, Lovecraft was taking the best from both sides of the Atlantic — the cosmicism of America, the cosmic inclinations of some British writers, the literary philosophy of Poe, and to some degree the heavy atmosphere of Victorian and Edwardian horror stories.

Among those whom Lovecraft admired was Matthew Phipps Shiel, three of whose stories are cited in "Supernatural Horror in Literature." Shiel's "Xelucha" is only faintly of the Lovecraftian cast. It deals with an archetypal seductress who acquaints the main character with the nature of man's place in the cosmos. Her haunting statement that "Pain is the sub-consciousness in conscious creatures of Eternity, and of loss," echoes not only Lovecraft's own philosophical pessimism but sounds also a bit like American Nathaniel Hawthorne's treatment of man as a tragic fallen character. Lovecraft also points to Shiel's "The House of Sounds," which "tells of a creeping horror and menace trickling down the centuries on a sub-arctic island," and *The Purple Cloud*, which deals with "a curse which came out of the arctic to destroy mankind." The plot idea of a gigantic monstrosity that descends upon an unwary world from the cold wastes is not unfamiliar to the reader of Lovecraft, who will recognize it as the basic substance of his "At the Mountains of Madness." At the same time, however, this novelette was primarily generated by Poe's "Narrative of A. Gordon Pym," although it is not impossible that both Shiel's and Lovecraft's tales may have sprung from a common source.

Shiel's works are relevant to Lovecraft's not only in their similarity of plot, though. As a member of Oscar Wilde's circle of artists, Shiel was bound to take delight in the ghoulish aesthetics of his writing. This is probably why his prose fiction more closely resembles poetry in its sound and movement, primarily because Shiel relies on elipses as a rhetorical device to create an uncanny atmosphere. "Xelucha," for example, is rather difficult to follow because Shiel deliberately leaves out the long narrative passages necessary to fill in the gaps left by the heavily philosophical dialogue. What we get are sporadic glimpses into the minds of the characters—glimpses of that which is revealed only in clipped dialogue. This may well be what led Lovecraft to call the story a fragment, and this disorienting confusion, combined with the terrible revelation about the nature of man's estate in the universe, produces a shock effect in the reader. It is that depression-laden atmosphere that would have attracted Lovecraft to Shiel's fiction as much as the themes and plot ideas, for, to Lovecraft, nothing was more important to weird fiction than atmosphere—choking, heavy, and capable of moving a reader profoundly.

The British poet Walter de la Mare also had some impact—of him Lovecraft states, "he is among the very few to whom unreality is a vivid, living presence." Here again is the notion of a surreal kind of dis- orientation, a confusion of events in which the unreal may become the real. And Lovecraft seems to be making a distinction between the simple willing suspension of disbelief and unreality's being "a vivid, living presence." For the weird tale to succeed, Lovecraft seems to imply, it must be invested with a quality that removes the reader en- tirely from the expectation of the commonplace and elevates him into a realm wherein the miraculous is the foundation.

In de la Mare, also, we find a number of stories whose titles and plots suggest Lovecraft stories. De la Mare's *The Return*, according to Lovecraft, has "the soul of a dead man reach out of its grave of two centuries and fasten itself upon the flesh of the living, so that even the face of the victim becomes that which had long ago turned to dust." Similar events also transpire in "The Case of Charles Dexter Ward" as the power of old Joseph Curwin creeps into the life of young Ward. "The Tree" by de la Mare concerns an unearthly plant that grows in "the yard of a starving artist," just as Lovecraft's tale "The Tree" concerns the role of a twisted plant in the not-so-friendly rivalry of two sculptors.

As a result of the British inclination to construct fantastic stories based on ancient mythology, the Greek fertility god Pan became a favorite subject in the 1890s. Lovecraft briefly mentions E. F. Benson's "The Man Who Went Too Far" as a tale of this type in which a dead man is found with the god's cloven hoofprint on his chest. The little- known author Huan Mee contributed "The God Pan" in 1896, and probably the most famous such story was Arthur Machen's "The

Great God Pan,'' which relates an erotically charged series of events that involve Pan's mating with a mortal woman in modern England.

The Pan theme apparently caught Lovecraft's imagination as well. We think almost automatically of ''The Dunwich Horror's'' goatish Wilbur Whateley, and we recall that those ceremonies of the Whateleys on Sentinel Hill during the nights of May Eve and Hallowe'en do in fact involve to some extent the mating of human beings with otherwordly monsters. Lovecraft also seems to have derived his powerful god Shub-Niggurath from the Pan prototype, because Shub-Niggurath is described as ''the Goat with a Thousand Young.'' The suggestion here is undeniably sinister, inferring as it does the geometric proliferation of monstrous entities on earth—all carried out under the aegis of the instinctively self-regenerating Pan figure in Lovecraft's pantheon.

It should be remarked, however, that while many of the British Pan stories carried veiled hints of the erotic, Lovecraft himself was so lukewarm on the subject of human sexuality that he would never have consciously invested his fiction with it. Nevertheless, it cannot be refuted that the fate of Lavinia Whateley in ''The Dunwich Horror'' is purely sexual in nature. And this tends to make that long story as close to eroticism as anything Lovecraft wrote—with the possible exception of ''The Thing on the Doorstep,'' in which Asenath Waite, wife of Edward Derby, comes forth ostensibly as a powerful female malefactor. One senses that the eroticism in ''The Dunwich Horror'' is very much like that of the Victorian and Edwardian periods in general, as these periods in history were characterized by a staid moral rectitude on the surface but boiled enough underneath to leave behind works like Frank Harris's *My Secret Life*. The point here is that while human civilization, represented by Victorian morality and by the proper behavior of the human heroes in Victorian horror stories, may strive consciously for moral action, there is always a darker side of reality, monstrous in nature, that is capable of subverting that aspiration.

Thus although Lovecraft may have considered sex to be a subject that genteel people did not even discuss, the sexual dimension is forced upon his characters—particularly in ''The Dunwich Horror''— and this becomes doubly loathsome. It is not only sex, but it is perverted, demonic sex.

Because Lovecraft was a contemporary of some of weird fiction's most notable authors, he establishes a separate section of ''Supernatural Horror in Literature'' in which to deal with them. ''The Modern

Masters" addresses itself to a number of Lovecraft's contempo-
raries — chiefly to four writers who had a great influence on him: Algernon Blackwood, Montague Rhodes James, Arthur Machen, and Lord
Dunsany.

Lovecraft finds much of the work of Blackwood to be "marred by
several defects such as ethical didacticism, occasional insipid whim-
sicality . . . and a too free use of the trade jargon of modern occultism." These qualities, Lovecraft feels, tend to undermine the creation
of a weird atmosphere by causing the reader's attention to atmospherical details to be distracted. Actually, Blackwood's use of "the
trade jargon of modern occultism" is fully to be expected since he was
a member of the British Order of the Golden Dawn, a society dedicated to the study and practice of ritual ceremonial magic. And it is
something of a tribute to writers like Machen, W. B. Yeats, Sax
Rohmer of Fu Manchu fame, and Robert Louis Stevenson that Lovecraft does not perceive a similar problem in them, since they were all at
one time or another associated with the order.

Of Blackwood's work, Lovecraft most highly esteems "The
Willows," "The Wendigo," "An Episode in a Lodging House," "The
Listener," and a volume of stories called *Incredible Adventures*, which
all share in common the theme of "unnamable presences" stumbled
upon by luckless individuals. Lovecraft rather grudgingly accepts the
John Silence series of stories that deal with a psychic detective, al-
though he finds them a bit too much in the cast of the Sherlock
Holmes tales to be truly successful as weird fiction.

There were two major aspects in the work of Montague Rhodes
James that Lovecraft found particularly attractive. The first was that
James deliberately eschewed technical occultism in favor of a more
prosaic approach against which to contrast his spectral occurrences,
and the second was that James was himself a great scholar and antiquarian just as Lovecraft was. Lovecraft delighted in the verisimilitude
with which James was able to invest his descriptions of ancient English cathedrals, for example, as James was an expert on British
cathedral history. Lovecraft admired also James's ability to depart
"considerably from the conventional Gothic tradition" in presenting
ghostly apparitions that were suggested rather than seen explicitly.
Lovecraft surely subscribed to this notion himself, for he is at his horrific best when he only hints at demonic presences rather than when
he describes them at length.

Paying tribute to James's best story, "Count Magnus," Lovecraft describes in detail virtually the entire plot line. Briefly, the plot concerns one Mr. Wraxall, who becomes fascinated with the entombed corpse of Count Magnus, a seventeenth-century landowner and practitioner of the occult. His interest having been too great and his proximity to the count's remains too close, Wraxall finds himself pursued by two cloaked figures, one of whom is almost certainly Magnus himself.

The notion of being followed by monsters was surely a part of Lovecraft's own fiction, since his tales are almost always infused with a sense of cosmic paranoia. And it should be noted that American writer Robert W. Chambers' classic story "The Yellow Sign" deals with a similar series of events, in which the main character has blundered onto a mysterious book and amulet that cause him to be watched at all hours by a cloaked figure who is his undoing. In fact, "The Yellow Sign" became a part of Lovecraft's mythos by dint of Lovecraft's appropriating the dreaded Yellow Sign itself for use in his own "Whisperer in Darkness."

Lovecraft's use of the classic British fascination with tombs and their contents may also have been derived most substantially from "Count Magnus," since Wraxall's interest in Magnus's mausoleum is seen in about the same form in Lovecraft's "The Tomb." However, Lovecraft may also have taken some of this morbid technique from a fellow American, F. Marion Crawford, whose forte seems to have been his ability to describe in the most gruesome detail the appearance of rotting, decomposing bodies. And this comes a bit closer to Lovecraft's suffocatingly atmospheric vignettes "In the Vault" and "Cool Air."

Those dozen or so Lovecraft stories that concern his Mythos pantheon of transdimensional monsters, however, show a clear, marked influence of the man whom Lovecraft seems to have considered the true giant of British weird fiction: Arthur Machen. Born in the Welsh village long held to be the location of King Arthur's Round Table court, Machen was an actor, author, mystic, and ceremonial magician. At an early age he became deeply interested in world mythology, particularly in that of the Greeks, Romans, and Celts. Much of this kind of mythology finds its way into his horror stories, which usually concern themselves with a magical universe, Platonic in nature, behind the outward reality of which there exist horrible forces and entities capable of exterminating mankind.

These themes show up most clearly in tales like "The Great God

Pan," in which a surgical experiment causes a woman, as Lovecraft puts it, "to see the vast and monstrous deity of Nature," and in Machen's other major fiction works, "The White People," "The Novel of the White Powder," "The Novel of the Black Seal," and "The Three Imposters." For Lovecraft, Machen's work probably provided an even greater source book for devices of plot than the work of Poe. From "The Great God Pan," as we have noted, it is likely that Lovecraft derived his own "god" Shub-Niggurath as well as the notion of the monster-spawn of "The Dunwich Horror." The repulsive conclusion of "The Novel of the White Powder" suggests also the demise of both Dr. Muñoz in "Cool Air" and of Edward Derby in "The Thing on the Doorstep." The truly startling scene in "The Novel of the Black Seal," in which a tentacle bursts from the stomach of a man obsessed with occult evil, relates directly to the similar physical peculiarity of Wilbur Whateley in "The Dunwich Horror." Even Machen's "The Three Imposters," which deals with the Gaelic myth of the Little People, may be traced through to Lovecraft's tales of subterranean burrowers such as "The Lurking Fear" and "Pickman's Model."

Another important point of comparison between Lovecraft and Machen is that Machen's fiction is often set against the wild, rural locale of England's moor country and in the desolate Welsh countryside villages. As any American who has traveled into the hills of Appalachia or the Ozarks knows, this dissociation from the comparatively well-ordered commonplaces of urban life opens up a whole world of possible action. Whereas Machen often used the lonely Welsh hills, Lovecraft sets many of his stories in isolated sections of Massachusetts, Vermont, and Maine. Even when Machen used London itself as a fictive locale, he wisely chose the less fashionable sections of the city, just as Lovecraft felt obliged to carry his action to Brooklyn's squalid waterfront district in "The Horror at Red Hook." In these settings terrific events may transpire observed by only a few—a technical necessity in really sound horror stories—and even when whole towns or large groups of people encounter occult experiences, there is always literary recourse to the people's conspiracy of silence. But the primary advantage in this kind of setting is that it represents a psychophysical landscape in which ancient, broken-down, unimproved architectural and topographical features mesh cleanly with the sense of archaicism and antiquity that surrounds Machen's and Lovecraft's spectral apparitions, the result being that the landscape works in concert with the thematic motif.

To Lovecraft, who, by the time he had written "Supernatural Horror in Literature," had already begun to envision a fictional supernatural world unified by a pantheon of gods and recurrent mystical signs and terms, there could have been no more important figure than Machen. Although Machen was an accomplished occultist himself, nevertheless he did not bog his fiction down with those hackneyed jargon terms associated with occult practice. Rather, he invented his own mystical terminology but took great care to refrain from explaining what it meant. In this way Machen's references to terms—for example, the "Aklo letters," "the Chian language," and "the voorish sign," mentioned in "The White People"—lent a ring of verisimilitude to his occult universe, yet shrouded it in mystery at the same time.

This practice so appealed to Lovecraft that he not only invented similar terms of his own but appropriated a few of Machen's for use in his own stories. Hence "the voorish sign" turns up in "The Dunwich Horror," and Machen's "Dols" appear in various spellings in "The Whisperer in Darkness," "The Dream-Quest of Unknown Kadath" and "Through the Gates of the Silver Key."

The last two stories mentioned here are members of that class of Lovecraft's work usually referred to as the dreamland tales. And just as Machen provided a kind of prototype for Lovecraft's Mythos pantheon stories, it was Edward John Moreton Drax Plunkett, the eighteenth Baron Dunsany—known to his readers as Lord Dunsany—who was most responsible for Lovecraft's dreamland stories. Unlike the rest of Lovecraft's fiction, the dreamland stories have nothing whatever to do with the familiar world of human history. Rather, they take place in worlds that never were, except in the magic labyrinths of the imagination, and Lovecraft's typical means of a character's ingress into these worlds is a kind of out-of-body travel that occurs during sleep. Sometimes the dreamland stories may involve frightening visions of other dimensions, but more often than not they represent sheer poetic escape from the banalities of everyday life—almost as if they were a form of therapeutic relaxation for their author.

Because Lovecraft had always been deeply moved by what he called Dunsany's "sorcery of crystalline singing prose" and his "creation of a gorgeous and languorous world of iridescently exotic vision," there was no hesitation on Lovecraft's part in admitting that his own dreamland stories were Dunsanian imitations. Many of his early tales were of the Dunsanian stamp, among them "The Doom That Came to Sarnath," "The White Ship," "The Cats of Ulthar," "The Other

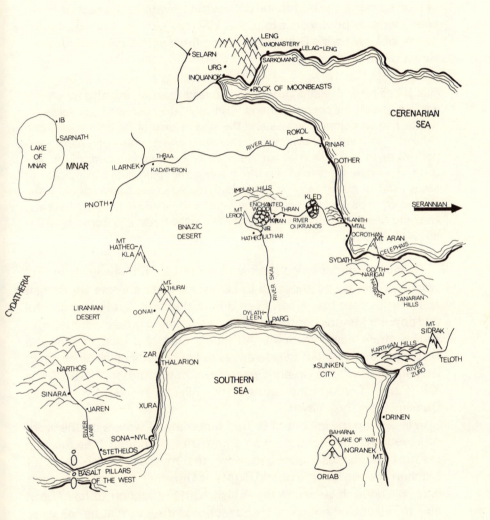

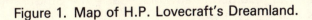

Figure 1. Map of H.P. Lovecraft's Dreamland.

Gods" and "The Quest of Iranon." These stories are characterized by densely poetic diction, fabulous settings, and wholly fantastic plot lines. Often they do not amount to much more than dreamy fragments or plotted vignettes and therefore seem to relate to the rest of Lovecraft's work as poetry does to prose. We may perhaps understand the nature of Lovecraft's Dunsanian fiction most easily if we note his observation that Dunsany:

stands dedicated to a strange world of fantastic beauty, and pledges eternal warfare against the coarseness and ugliness of diurnal reality. . . . As sensitive as Poe to dramatic values and the significance of isolated words and details . . . this author draws with tremendous effectiveness on nearly every body of myth and legend within the circle of European culture. . . . In *The Book of Wonder* we read of Hlo-Hlo, the gigantic spider-idol which does not always stay at home; of what the Sphinx feared in the forest; of Slith, the thief who jumps over the edge of the world after seeing a certain light lit and knowing *who* lit it . . . of the Gnoles, who live in the forest and from whom it is not well to steal . . . .

These sometimes lyrical, sometimes horrible, but always beautiful worlds of fantasy so appealed to Lovecraft that he wrote Dunsanian tales throughout his career. Even during the time that his successful and popular Mythos pantheon stories were being produced, the Dunsanian strain came through. Although there are elements of the Mythos in them by dint of references to Lovecraft's patheon of gods, later stories like "The Dream-Quest of Unknown Kadath," "The Silver Key," and "Through the Gates of the Silver Key" remain basically Dunsanian in their flavor.

In assessing the impact of British supernatural writers on the work of Lovecraft, therefore, we can summarize by noting that the two greatest influences upon him were the mystical Welsh tales of Machen and the fanciful poetic flights of Dunsany. Further, Lovecraft was well enough versed in the British horrific tradition to have been able to select elements of plot and technical devices that he felt were literarily sound. By becoming initimately acquainted with the conventions of gothicism, Lovecraft was able to eschew it, or at least to modify it for his own purposes, weeding out its clichés and avoiding what he sensed to be its glibness. He found that it was possible to model his literary style successfully upon several outstanding British writers and to incorporate advantageously the British ambience of antiquity into his own work.

But of primary importance to Lovecraft's place in literary history is the plain fact that he was not British. His imitation of Dunsany in writing the dreamland stories was perfectly functional. But unless he were to adopt British landscape and mythology for his stories that were grounded in this world, and thereby become a British writer himself, Lovecraft would have to face the same problem that Nathaniel Hawthorne had confronted seventy years earlier. He would have to discover a usable American past that suited his necessity for archaism. Since America had no ruined castles or ancient legends of Little People or fairies, Lovecraft had to look into what antiquity America did have to offer and from there utilize, modify, amplify, and amend what he found. He also had to study the literary tradition of his own country in order to see how his efforts might be a part of the overall scheme.

LOVECRAFT AND THE AMERICAN FANTASTIC IDEAL

Much of the vitality of the literary tradition in America is derived from its being so intimately bound up in the horrific, the speculative, and the fantastic. It seems that a long, dark shadow of fantasy has always lain across our national literature—from the devil- and witch-ridden forests of the New England Puritans right up to the most contemporary American fabulists such as Kurt Vonnegut, Jr., Robert Coover, and Donald Barthelme. Along the way we have had the gothic tales of Charles Brockden Brown, the New York Dutch fantasies of Irving, the dark allegories of Hawthorne, and the more philosophical terror of Melville. Poe acquainted American literature with "the grim phantasm FEAR," and Oliver Wendell Holmes worked out his serpentine imagery in *Elsie Venner*. The nihilistic Ambrose Bierce, "Bitter Bierce" as he was sometimes called, produced what were perhaps the most caustic and cynical horror stories of the post-Civil War period.

Even when T. S. Eliot admitted us to the wasteland of the twentieth century, we found ourselves moving through a bizarre landscape that was at once strange and familiar. And it is certainly significant that one of the greatest American novels about the tragic defect in our national character, which we have come to call "the American Dream," was Fitzgerald's *The Great Gatsby*, the story of a man who inhabits a dream world almost exclusively, a dream world that is his undoing.

To say that H. P. Lovecraft was a part of this literary and intellectual mainstream would be in error; his literary intent was essentially only to write tales of terror. But it would be equally erroneous to suggest that Lovecraft was not affected by the mainstream's currents or to say that there is nothing American about his work. In fact, Lovecraft's fiction, and particularly his late or mature fiction, is very American in character.

Lovecraft was raised by his mother and then his two aunts in the essential belief that he was a kind of aristocrat, that is, a gentleman of an old New England family who did not associate with the rabble. It is reasonable to assume, therefore, that he was to some degree divorced from the mainstream of American life. It would not, however, be reasonable to say that the Puritan morality that still influences most Americans did not influence Lovecraft as well. It is just that in Lovecraft's life and fiction that influence manifested itself in a way different from those of other major American writers.

Throughout American history, the simplistic Puritan dichotomy of good against evil, black versus white, as it was often symbolized, caused a kind of national neurosis. The tension created by this Manichean division has shown itself from Puritan times to the present in the notion that what is not godly, or good at least, is automatically shameful or wicked. While Lovecraft subscribed for much of his life to the idea that blacks were an inferior race and that the luridness of sex had no place in the minds of genteel people, the dark-versus-light dichotomy is not used in a Puritan manner in his fiction.

Although the dark-light metaphor appears regularly throughout American literature, the two greatest writers to make use of it were Hawthorne and Melville. Hawthorne's bleak tales employed this Puritan notion to deepen our understanding of the principles of dark and light that exist in every human heart quite independent of any external God or devil. The God or devil of men is of their own creation and depends upon what choices a man makes within his own sphere of experience. Hawthorne felt that human beings usually opt for wicked choices, those that are ruinous of love and destructive to any warmth that humans might share in an impossibly difficult world.

For Melville the dark-light imagery took on universal proportions and finally became contradictory and ambiguous. It is the dark Captain Ahab who hunts the White Whale, but Ahab sees Moby Dick as inscrutably malevolent and wishes to destroy him. Through it all the whale, whom Ishmael has described as ghastly in its whiteness for a variety of philosophical reasons, seems to remain benign, or at least resists the reader's attempts to understand it as good or evil.

But the point is that for both of these writers, the dark-light conflict exists within the personalities or the souls of the major characters. In Lovecraft it is different. Here the theme of good versus evil within the hero usually does not surface—and when it does, it is in the form of a shocking recognition of the existence of evil alone (as in Charles Dexter Ward's being obsessed by the spirit of his ancestor Joseph Curwin), a condition that often drives the main character to suicide, as with Arthur Jermyn. Normally, however, the evil experienced by Lovecraft's main characters is external to them and is pervasive in the world. This causes a terrible understanding of the nature of things, which, once again, may lead to suicide.

In this respect, Lovecraft is strikingly modern. The sense of being alone and afraid in a world one never made is common among many writers of the twentieth century. We shall probably never know whether or not Lovecraft was making an apt pun in the title of "Arthur Jermyn"—whether or not he was trying to tell his readers just how germane this tale is to his thinking. But it surely is.

In the first paragraph of the story, Lovecraft writes that:

Science, already oppressive with its shocking revelations, will perhaps be the ultimate exterminator of our human species—if separate species we be—for its reserve of unguessed horrors could never be borne by mortal brains if loosed upon the world. If we knew what we are, we should do as Arthur Jermyn did; and Arthur Jermyn soaked himself in oil and set fire to his clothing one night.

This is a singularly powerful and affecting passage. It has all of the brutal and forceful frontal-attack qualities that one might associate with a photograph of an assassination, as well as the lean, spare, tough literary technique found in the best twentieth-century writers.

If all this sounds prophetic of our own times on Lovecraft's part, we should keep in mind that it is not. Between the years 1900 and 1905, the world, as it had been known up to that time, simply ceased to exist. During this period, the Wright Brothers flew their gasoline-powered aeroplane at Kitty Hawk, Sigmund Freud published *On the Interpretations of Dreams*, a book that shattered man's image of himself, and Albert Einstein brought the great age of Newtonian physics to an end with the publication of his *Special Theory of Relativity*.

Lovecraft, of course, was keenly interested in science, and by the time he came to write those lines in "Arthur Jermyn," he had already witnessed, as had so many others, the horrors of the Great War—a war so terrible that it was thought by some to be man's final war. The world of 1900 through 1920 was a world that seemed to be falling apart, a chaos that pointed the way toward Armageddon. In "Arthur Jermyn," a story of a human being who had not quite "let go the hot gorilla's paw" (as Ray Bradbury put it in *Something Wicked This Way Comes*), Lovecraft was simply responding sensitively and cynically to the world that he saw.

There are two biographical factors here that are important. First, there was Lovecraft's physical isolation from the outside world, a situation that must have profoundly deepened his acid scorn for the human race and the doomed world it inhabits. And second, although raised in a Puritanical home and influenced psychologically by it to his very roots, Lovecraft was affected enough by modern science to have become an agnostic. With the removal of a religious framework in terms of which to see a redemptive moral salvation for man, things must have seemed pointless and bleak indeed.

The question may arise as to whether or not Lovecraft's strange half-breeds, the offspring of horrible liaisons between men and monsters, can be seen as a return to the nineteenth-century tension between dark and light principles existing simultaneously in a human being. Here we may think of the people of Innsmouth, of Dunwich's Wilbur Whately, of Arthur Jermyn himself. But we seem to arrive once again at the pessimistic conclusion. In these characters, though mixtures of men and monsters, it is the evil of the monster and the evil of the human parent that survive. In those cases in which Lovecraft surrounds a decent and pure main character (many of his first-person narrators are modeled upon himself) with wicked ones, it is the sheer enormity of the world's evil pitted against the pitiful insignificance of the hero's good that drives the hero into madness or actually into removing himself from the world by violence. There is a clearly perceivable paranoia in this version of reality.

Finally, and this is perhaps the most insidious dimension of Lovecraft's work, we come to understand that if we are looking for a moral, we might just as well forget it. There is none. This was a view taken by the post-Civil War naturalists who wrote in the generation preceding Lovecraft's. Represented by literary artists such as Stephen Crane, Jack London, Frank Norris, and Ambrose Bierce, the naturalists saw the universe as a blind, dead, uncaring beast that occasionally blundered against men and, without any particular malice, exterminated them. This kind of thing happens often in Lovecraft, particularly in the earlier stories like "The Other Gods," in which it is the encounter with monsters, which are only innocently going about their business of being monsters, that destroys men.

In the later stories, however, the monsters do take on malevolent characteristics and become creatures whose design it is to wipe out mankind and inherit the earth. This notion is pure survival-of-the-fittest philosophy (which is to say in this case survival of the most powerful), another scientific idea that rocked the world and has been around in one form or another ever since.

One way, therefore, that Lovecraft's literary career might be categorized is by dividing it according to whether or not the forces of nature and supernature that appear in the stories operate through naturalistic impersonality or through conscious evil intent. It is generally in the early stories that we find the former and in the later Mythos pantheon stories that we find the latter. This method of division, of course, does not account for many of the pure fantasy-land or dream stories, such as "The Doom That Came to Sarnath," which, as we have seen, conform to the Dunsanian poetic principle.

Of the prodigious amount of writing that Lovecraft did, it was surely his so-called Cthulhu Mythos for which he became most famous. Briefly, the Mythos consists of a series of a dozen or so stories, interrelated but not interdependent, that are based upon a common, central theme. The idea is that before man ever evolved upon the earth, a race of creatures that Lovecraft called the Great Old Ones came here from deep space to rule. But they were essentially demonic in nature, and when man came upon the earth, they subjugated him. Some men in turn fell to worshiping these creatures. Subsequently, the Old Ones lapsed in their rule and either fell into a dreamless slumber in the earth's remote places or vanished into other dimensions of space and time.

But the seed of evil had either been planted in man by the Old Ones, or it had existed already. In any case, by using certain horrible rituals that survived from the Old Ones' reign on earth, small enclaves of human beings remained dedicated to the Old Ones, virtually forming a religion on the basis of their return. And it was through those surviving rituals found in books like the *Necronomicon* that the Old Ones' reinheritance of the earth could be effected.

This theory is particularly well developed in "The Case of Charles Dexter Ward," in which Lovecraft suggests that every element of what we have come to call the black arts has its roots in the ritual veneration of these monsters from space. And the theory is especially provocative and intriguing in that it attempts to unify and attribute a common cause to human superstition and occultism—something that certain psychologists and anthropologists have been trying to do for years anyway.

A point to take into consideration here is the naming of the Cthulhu Mythos. Actually, Lovecraft himself never used this term, referring instead only to his "Cthulhuism" or "Yog-Sothothery." The term "Cthulhu Mythos" was only invented, or at least came into popular use, after his death. This was largely the doing of his literary friends and disciples. We ought to remember, however, that in the pantheon of gods that Lovecraft incorporated into his Mythos, Cthulhu was only the sea god who dwelt in the submarine depths of R'lyeh, an Atlantis-like setting. Other gods include Yog-Sothoth (hence, "Yog-Sothothery"), Shub-Niggurath, Azathoth, and Nyarlathotep.

All of these creatures are mentioned in one or more stories, but it is only in "The Call of Cthulhu" that Cthulhu actually appears. The reason, then, for naming the myth cycle after Cthulhu is a bit of a mystery. And it is really a trifle unfortunate, since it not only underplays the importance of the others (like Yog-Sothoth, whose offspring rips up the countryside in "The Dunwich Horror") but also tends to distract us from one truly significant element that most of the stories have in common—the New England setting.

Although the list of stories that can be considered Mythos tales varies from critic to critic, it can hardly be disallowed that the majority of them take place against the Puritan setting of Lovecraft's beloved New England. The use of the term "Cthulhu Mythos" draws our attention away from this fact (in "The Call of Cthulhu" the monster appears in the South Seas) and directs us either to Cthulhu's watery domain or to the god himself.

But, as we shall see, Lovecraft's use of the New England setting is of paramount importance to his literary theory, and it is for this reason that we probably ought to use the term "New England Mythos" to refer to that particular series of stories. However, to avoid needless confusion this series will be referred to here simply as the Mythos stories. And whether New England or Cthulhu, the Mythos stories surely stand independent of generic controversy.

One of the traditional criteria that scholars and critics of literature (and particularly of American literature) have applied to determine the merit of a serious writer's work is to consider to what extent that writer understood the literary history of which he was a part. Here, specifically, we are dealing with Lovecraft not only as a writer of fantastic fiction but of American fantastic fiction.

Of remarkable significance to this study of Lovecraft's literary theory is his observation that "Quite alone as both a novel and a piece of terror-literature stands the famous *Wuthering Heights* (1847) by Emily Brontë, with its mad vistas of bleak, wind-swept Yorkshire moors and the violent, distorted lives they foster." From this it is obvious that setting is highly integral to plot in Lovecraft's estimation. Furthermore, holding *Wuthering Heights* in such high esteem, singling it out from other British Romantic literature, has been a kind of preoccupation with American writers and critics, for the elements of American romance are nowhere more evident in a British novel than in Bronte's book. These elements would include the large-scale setting of the open moor country and the skillful commingling of the actual and the imaginary to a point where it is difficult for the reader to discern the difference.

In grappling with the problem of American horror fiction, Lovecraft includes a lengthy section in "Supernatural Horror in Literature" entitled "The Weird Tradition in America," which contains full and detailed discussions of Nathaniel Hawthorne and Ambrose Bierce, whom Lovecraft considered of particular importance to the genre. The one notable figure missing in this discussion is Herman Melville, author of *Moby-Dick*, with its diabolism and satanic implications, as well as of a number of short stories that qualify as weird fiction. But this may be accounted for when we remember that *Moby-Dick*, one of the greatest and most profound American novels, was not recognized as anything but a sea story until the early twentieth century, and at the time Lovecraft wrote his essay, little critical work had been done on the book.

Lovecraft does indicate his familiarity with some American literary criticism, however, since he cites the scholar Paul Elmer More in the essay's examination of Hawthorne. Lovecraft had probably read the two excellent essays on Hawthorne in More's famous *Shelburne Essays in American Literature*, and later Lovecraft was able to mobilize D. H. Lawrence's observations about Hawthorne from his *Studies in Classic American Literature*. What this shows is that Lovecraft was not simply making idle, armchair, belletristic observations about American literature but had engaged in its serious study.

Paraphrasing More's work, Lovecraft perceptively points to the all-important cultural context into which American literature was born. America was, he says, deeply marked by "keen spiritual and theological interests" from the time of the first Separatist landing at Plymouth Rock. This, coupled with the desolate scene of virgin wilderness into which the Separatists had been carried by the *Mayflower*, caused the Puritan leader William Bradford to write that his people felt cut off — three thousand miles of ocean behind them and in front of them "a hideous and desolate wilderness, full of wild beasts and wild men . . . . For summer being done, all things stand upon them with a weather-beaten face, and the whole country, full of woods and thickets, represented a wild and savage hue." Bradford noted that under such circumstances the Puritans could turn their eyes only upward toward heaven, and this represents the first American impulse to escape physical reality for a spiritual reality, and established the propensity to transcend to finer, more shining worlds.

The Puritans considered that much of what was earthly was satanic. In this way the Indians were associated with the devil, and the conditions were set up under which operated the celebrated Salem witchcraft trials and executions that weighed so heavily on Hawthorne, whose own ancestor had been one of the prosecutors. Hawthorne himself did not believe in these Puritan interpretations of nature, but he did use them symbolically in his investigation of man's moral constitution. Lovecraft's judgment is wholly correct that Hawthorne

grieved at an unmoral universe which everywhere transcends the conventional patterns thought by our forefathers to represent divine and immutable law. Evil, a very real force to Hawthorne, appears on every hand as a lurking, conquering adversary; and the visible world becomes in his fancy a theatre of infinite tragedy and woe, with unseen half-existent influences hovering over and through it, battling for supremacy and moulding the destinies of the hapless mortals who form its vain and self-deluded population. *The heritage of American weirdness was his to a most intense degree, and he saw a dismal throng of vague spectres behind the common phenomona of life.* . . . [My italics.]

This Platonic notion of a shadowy world beyond or behind common day-to-day occurrences runs as a strong current throughout American literature. Lovecraft was not only wise to observe it but knew enough about its literary validity to use it in his own fiction. The demonic cults and hidden evils that fester behind the façade of those New England villages in his stories are a clear manifestation of his use of this philosophical concept.

For Lovecraft, "foremost as a finished, artistic unit among all our author's weird material is the famous and exquisitely wrought novel, *The House of Seven Gables.* . . ." Actually, this, like Hawthorne's other three long fiction works, is by definition not a novel, but a Romance. In defining the Romance genre, Hawthorne wrote in "The Custom-House" that the Romance establishes "a neutral territory, somewhere between the real world and fairy-land, where the Actual and the Imaginary may meet and each imbue itself with the nature of the other." In the preface to *The House of Seven Gables* Hawthorne adds that a writer of Romance "wishes to claim a certain latitude, both as to its fashion and material, which he would not have felt himself entitled to assume had he professed to be writing a Novel." The Romance writer may "so manage his atmospherical medium as to bring out or mellow the lights and deepen and enrich the shadows of the picture." In Lovecraft, too, it is the skillful management of "his atmospherical medium" that makes the stories so successful as vehicles for drawing out hidden and uncertain sensations of fear.

In the twilight world of the Romance it is precisely what one does not see, or rather what one is uncertain about seeing, that lends to it an atmosphere of terror. In Hawthorne's "Young Goodman Brown," for example, Brown never actually sees a witch flying on a broomstick as he travels through the forest on his way to a witch's sabbath. The old man who is his guide carries a walking stick that *seems* to turn into a serpent, but in the half-light Brown cannot be certain. Similarly, in Lovecraft it is often what he does not tell us that creates the uncanny atmosphere. Lovecraft's weakest moments tend to be those in which he describes a monster visually; and his strongest ones, those in which he only hints dimly at what may be lurking nearby. Like the rampant imaginations of Hawthorne's guilt-ridden characters, the imaginations of Lovecraft's readers fill in what Lovecraft has deliberately left out, but they fill it in vaguely, so that they themselves may not be quite aware of what is causing their uneasiness.

Unlike Hawthorne, however, Lovecraft was little interested in dealing with life on a moral level, except in isolated instances such as in "The White Ship," which is a moral allegory, pure and simple, based on *Pilgrim's Progress* and possibly on Hawthorne's "The Celestial Railroad." Hawthorne's theme of ancestral evil descending upon an unfortunate victim who must then wrestle with the moral issue becomes transmuted in Lovecraft. Although he uses this idea in many of his stories, he uses it as the stimulus that evokes only terror in his main characters. Usually, in Lovecraft's mature work, the main characters find themselves caught in a universe of cosmic conspiracy, in a world that is impossibly evil and bent only on the destruction of men. In this way Lovecraft's fiction becomes strangely nihilistic, akin to that of Bierce.

Bierce, who wandered into Mexico in 1913 and was never seen again, is best remembered for his tales of horror and his bitter Civil War stories. In the latter category the best known are "An Occurrence at Owl Creek Bridge," "Chickamauga" and "One of the Missing," social and psychological antiwar statements both grim and upsetting. Of his horror stories "The Damned Thing" is perhaps most often read, and it is in this tale that Lovecraft sees Bierce's sense of "inhumanity" finding "vent in a rare strain of sardonic comedy and graveyard humour." An example, says Lovecraft, is illustrated in the subtitles, "such as 'One does not always eat what is on the table,' describing a body laid out for a coroner's inquest, and 'A man though naked may be in rags,' referring to a frightfully mangled corpse."

These philosophical questions aside, however, it was to Poe that Lovecraft owed the most as a prose stylist and Poe whom he revered more than any other American writer. In "Supernatural Horror in Literature" Lovecraft devotes an entire section to Poe, which occurs between "Special Literature on the Continent" and "The Weird Tradition in America," suggesting not only the importance of Poe, but also that he was Lovecraft's link between Europe (where Poe was appreciated and read during his lifetime) and America.

Lovecraft saw Poe as rising to heights of "cosmic terror" far above that which was achieved by any other author of weird fiction, adding that it was "to our good fortune as Americans" to be able to claim Poe as our own. The great similarities between Poe and Lovecraft form the kelson of Lovecraft's literary theory and thus demand scrutiny here.

Fortunately, in addition to his fiction and poetry Poe also wrote "The Philosophy of Composition," an excellent essay on his own literary theory. In that essay Poe notes that fiction writing usually begins with a thesis or a basic idea for a plot, and this, in turn, is filled in "with description, dialogue, or authorial comment. . . ." Poe, however, prefers "commencing with the consideration of an *effect*." Poe says to himself, "'Of the innumerable effects, or impressions, of which the heart, the intellect, or (more generally) the soul is susceptible, what one on the present occasion shall I select?'" The effect on his readers of a story or poem, he decides, must be *"universally* apreciable."

In an all-important definitive passage, Poe observes:

That pleasure which is at once the most intense, the most elevating, and the most pure, is, I believe, found in the contemplation of the Beautiful. When, indeed, men speak of beauty, they mean, precisely, not a quality, as is supposed, but an effect—they refer, in short, just to that intense and pure elevation of *soul, not* of intellect, or of heart. . . . which is experienced in consequence of contemplating "the beautiful."

"Beauty," Poe maintains, "is the excitement, or pleasurable elevation, of the soul."

But for Poe the soul's elevation being pleasurable did not preclude the aesthetic experience of fear or unhappiness, since even these excite and elevate the soul to new levels of sensation. Therefore, Poe concludes that if this elevation of the soul must be universally appreciated, he should employ a tone in his work that is the summit of spiritual excitation. This, he believes, is sadness. The next question is: Of all melancholy topics which is the most melancholy? His answer is "the death of a beautiful woman," since death and sexual beauty are likely to provoke the greatest sympathetic reaction in the reader. Hence we have "The Raven," "Ligeia," and "The Fall of the House of Usher," all of which reflect this concept.

Poe then builds upon the concept by choosing just the imagery and the heavy, Latinate phrasing framed by the proper plot structure to convey the effect he has chosen. Like the artistic Prince Prospero in "The Masque of the Red Death," Poe himself has that "wonderful eye for colors and effects" that combine subtly to affect the reader. In "The Fall of the House of Usher," for example, it is Roderick Usher's obsession with fear ("the grim phantasm FEAR," he calls it) that culminates in the reader's own experience of fear.

Lovecraft has been much criticized for his apparent disinterest in strong, flashy elements of plot. Indeed, plot is sometimes so de-emphasized that one may read forty pages or so of one of the longer stories in the course of which nothing much happens. But Lovecraft well understood what he was about. These long passages often amount to virtually Henry James-like descriptions of the main character's psychological state or are given to physical depictions of setting. And it is this, rather than plot, that contributes to the total effect in Lovecraft's fiction. By focusing analytically on a man whose psychological state is deteriorating, Lovecraft is echoing Poe's treatment of the mind of Roderick Usher, and this technique casts an eerie and ghastly shadow over the entire work.

As an aside here, a basic difference between Poe and Lovecraft should be noted. While for Poe the most effective emotional theme was the death of a beautiful woman, Lovecraft almost completely eschewed the introduction of women into his fiction. The only story wherein a woman figures prominently is "The Thing on the Doorstep," and actually it is only Asenath Waite's physical presence that is the vehicle for horror, not any malevolence of the feminine mind. There has been a great deal of speculation about latent homosexuality on Lovecraft's part because of his disinclination to write about women. But this theory is better left in the hands of armchair psychologists and Freudian critics. A far more plausible reason for Lovecraft's aversion may be found in his Puritan upbringing and his lack of experience with women. After all, it is fairly difficult to write about something to which one has had little exposure and that one simply does not understand.

Following the lead of both Poe and Hawthorne, Lovecraft also came to understand the absolute importance of setting in achieving an overall effect. Hawthorne had struggled with the problem of a usable American setting in which the romance landscape could be constructed. He firmly believed that settings had to be in concert with the weird psychophysical action of a story or long fiction work. But America, he lamented, was simply too young a nation to have the appropriate gothic appurtenances necessary for the Romance. Nevertheless, Hawthorne reached for as dark and ancient a past as he could find. It was natural for him to use the haunted, half-lit world of the New England Puritans as setting. Poe, rather than resorting to New England, preferred to dislocate his setting in space and time, remaining unclear about just where the action was taking place.

Lovecraft borrowed from both authors, sometimes, like Poe, employing a setting "out of Space and out of Time," or, like Hawthorne, using colonial New England as his fantastic frame of reference. This latter impulse is what gave rise to Lovecraft's inventing the wild, desolate villages of Arkham, Kingsport, Dunwich, and Innsmouth as fictive locales. And it is these settings, as much as any monster-god he created, that have captured the imagination of his followers. Lovecraft's repetitive use of these settings has indeed had such an effect as to convince many readers that they are real places. That Arkham or Dunwich cannot be found on a roadmap of Massachusetts is a common, confused observation of the neophyte reader of Lovecraft.

Finally, every bit as important as setting and the psychological examination of characters is Lovecraft's rhetorical style. It was, perhaps, through his attempts to imitate the heavily ornate style of Poe, as well as his exposure to British literature, that Lovecraft found himself given to immensely complex sentence structure and an archaic vocabulary. It has been said that readers are simply unable to deal with this, a charge also leveled at Henry James. Actually, Lovecraft almost certainly had less control over his diction than either Poe or James did, and his adjectival explosions and archaicisms often make his fiction sound a bit silly by comparison. What must be kept in mind here is not the frequent awkwardness and heavy-handedness of a given passage or set of passages but, rather, the cumulative *effect* of Lovecraft's stories — their weirdness, which is precisely what he wanted them to be invested with.

Perhaps this quality simply defies analysis; perhaps we should not analyze it. It should, however, be sufficient to say that it is exactly Lovecraft's rhetorical excesses that make his style consistent with his characters who feel madness growing on them against the backdrop of macabre, otherworldly settings. And this is the reason that strangely, and often against our will, we begin to feel that Lovecraft is not writing fiction, but a hideous version of truth.

In terms of Lovecraft's philosophical conception of his own work, then, we may see that he derived his understanding of what weird fiction must do primarily from Poe, and his sense of a usable American past and of a workable psychophysical landscape from Hawthorne's theory of the Romance. But in a larger way Lovecraft's most important contribution to the overall framework of American literature was not altogether derivative. In the early twentieth century, a time when the older modes of literary thought were crumbling and when a writer like Hemingway could successfully machine-gun his readers with staccato diction and syntax, Lovecraft stood firmly in the midst of a syntax that was meant to be woven magically around the reader. And although the fantastic strain in American literature will probably always exist in one form or another, the Romance form in America as it was understood and practiced by both Hawthorne and Poe all but vanished with Lovecraft's death. Lovecraft was the last American writer to guide us, in the nineteenth-century tradition, on a fearful torchlight tour of witch-haunted New England.

LOVECRAFT'S LITERARY CIRCLE

In 1923 a periodical known as *Weird Tales* was born in Chicago. The editors referred to it as "the unique magazine," and in fact it was just that. While there were many other pulp magazines devoted to science fiction during the thirty-one years of *Weird Tales'* existence, this particular magazine was virtually alone in publishing horror and fantasy fiction of a consistently high literary quality.

The immediate impact and overall effect of *Weird Tales* on contemporary horror and fantasy were and are enormous. Not only was it the preeminent forum for weird fiction, but it was also the market that displayed some of the first major publications of the twentieth century's greatest horror and fantasy writers. Among those whose early work appeared in the magazine were Ray Bradbury, Robert Bloch, Fritz Leiber, Manley Wade Wellman, Frank Belknap Long, Robert E. Howard, H. Warner Munn, C. L. Moore, Henry Kuttner, and many, many others. Even Tennessee Williams managed to place a story there, entitled "The Vengeance of Nitocris."

Under the editorship, first, of Edwin F. Baird, who bought the first five Lovecraft stories to appear in *Weird Tales*, and then of the great Farnsworth Wright, who guided *Weird Tales* until 1940, the magazine came to be the literary gathering place for what was to be known as the Lovecraft Circle. Basic channels of communication were opened between the book's readers and its writers primarily as a result of the section called "The Eyrie"—the letters department. Lovecraft, voluminous correspondent that he was, contributed often to "The Eyrie" and was never loathe to respond to the interested comments and queries of his fans. This was the way, for example, that Lovecraft struck up a friendship with H. Warner Munn, the fantasist of Athol, Massachusetts, whom Lovecraft visited often. It was with Munn that Lovecraft traveled to the archeological site at Mystery Hill, New Hampshire, where, according to Munn himself, Lovecraft wandered among the stone ruins discoursing about his pantheon of timeless gods and how the monolithic setting would have well suited them.

Since Lovecraft did not often journey outside of New England, many of his best friendships existed almost wholly through correspondence. Lovecraft spent more of his time in writing letters than he did in writing fiction, and this was his means of contact with close literary associates like Texan Robert E. Howard, whose ferocious, swash-buckling adventures of Conan the Barbarian caused Lovecraft to nick-name him "Two-Gun Bob"; Californian Clark Ashton Smith, inventor of the Commorion myth cycle of frozen Hyperboria and namesake of Lovecraft's high priest Klarkash-Ton; and two young, aspiring weird-fiction writers from Wisconsin, Robert Bloch and August Derleth.

To this list of the original Lovecraft inner circle of major weird-fiction writers, one must, of course, add Frank Belknap Long, whom Lovecraft got to know well while living in New York City, and another midwesterner, Henry Kuttner, often best remembered for his science fiction collaborations with his wife, Catherine L. Moore. (Moore, it might be noted here, remains today one of the very best prose stylists in the weird-fiction genre.)

These seven people — Lovecraft, Howard, Smith, Long, Bloch, Der-leth, and Kuttner — together formed an unstructured alliance that was responsible for contributing over forty tales to Lovecraft's increasingly popular Mythos cycle, and it was Derleth who almost single-handedly brought Lovecraft to the attention of readers outside the pages of *Weird Tales*.

The Lovecraft purist might say that the only authentic Mythos stories were those that Lovecraft himself wrote — the tales concerning the pantheon of demonic gods, those with references to Abdul Alhaz-red's *Necronomicon* and other underground occult works like the *Pnakotic Manuscripts* and *R'lyeh Texts*, those frequently set in the rotting New England villages of Arkham, Dunwich, Kingsport, and Innsmouth. But the fact remains that Lovecraft's Mythos was so in-tellectually captivating that his friends could hardly refrain from add-ing to it. Indeed, Lovecraft himself encouraged them to do so. So it was in 1928, the year Lovecraft wrote "The Dunwich Horror," that what may have been the first Mythos story from another hand was published.

The story was Frank Belknap Long's "The Space Eaters," in which the main characters, Howard (a writer of weird fiction clearly modeled on Lovecraft) and Frank (presumably Long) encounter an ancient entity from space that eats into the brains of its victims. "The Space Eaters" was followed in 1929 by another Mythos tale from Long, his famous "Hounds of Tindalos." In this tale a student of philosophy and horror writer, Halpin Chalmers, discovers that horrible transdimensional Hound monsters can be admitted into this world through certain quirks of geometry — an idea that Lovecraft had used often, particularly in "Dreams in the Witch-House."

Following Lovecraft's formula, Long not only invented two new sets of monsters for inclusion into the Mythos pantheon, the Space Eaters and the Hounds of Tindalos, but he contributed a new rural setting, the town of Partridgeville. In "The Hounds" Long also made use of the "Doels," monsters taken from the works of Machen that were also mentioned by Lovecraft.

The year 1931 saw the publication of four new Mythos stories: "The Return of the Sorcerer" and "The Tale of Satampra Zeiros" by Clark Ashton Smith as well as "The Black Stone" and "The Children of the Night" by Robert E. Howard.

"The Return of the Sorcerer" concerns John Carnby, a student and practitioner of the occult, who is desperately studying the *Necronomicon* in an attempt to discover the cause of and cure for a gruesome spectral phenomenon that haunts him. "The Tale of Satampra Zeiros," a part of Smith's Hyperborian myth cycle and much more typical of his introspective, poetic prose, tells of a thief who determines to steal the jewels of a line of ancient kings. Though this story is set in Smith's fantasy-land, it nevertheless becomes a part of Lovecraft's Mythos through its introduction of the god Tsathoggua, which, like many of Lovecraft's deities, is an extraterrestrial that came to earth, in this case, from the planet Saturn. Lovecraft was impressed enough with Smith's newly invented god that he made mention of Tsathoggua in "At the Mountains of Madness," "The Shadow Out of Time," "Through the Gates of the Silver Key," and in "The Whisperer in Darkness." Hence the god became firmly entrenched in Lovecraft's pantheon.

Robert E. Howard's contributions to the Mythos were more traditionally along the Lovecraft line, since Howard was greatly devoted to the study of racial history and ancient myth patterns. This knowledge is exploited in both "The Black Stone" and "The Children of the Night." In the former story the narrator sets off for the Balkans in an effort to locate a fabled dark monument said to have horrible associations. It is the narrator's misfortune to discover the stone and to figure out what it means — and what appears on it certain nights of the year. "The Children of the Night" was probably a story more to Howard's personal liking, because it deals with barbaric and even sadistic feats of daring. Here, a blow on the head from a prehistoric adze catapults the narrator back in time to penetrate the secret of Britain's legendary Little People. There is a great deal of bloodshed, and even when the narrator returns to his own time in history, he is not the same man.

Howard's Mythos stories were notable for their grounding in established mythology and anthropology as well as for his invention of another mad poet, Justin Geoffrey, whose hideous poetic work *The People of the Monolith* Lovecraft worked into "The Thing on the Doorstep," as well as von Junzt's *Unaussprechlichen Kulten*, or *Nameless Cults*, which is mentioned in "Dreams in the Witch-House," "The Haunter of the Dark," "The Shadow Out of Time" and "The Thing on the Doorstep."

By now a pattern was being formed in the various non-Lovecraftian contributions to the Mythos. After the manner of Lovecraft, it was apparently necessary not only to mention the *Necronomicon* or one of Lovecraft's gods, but one had to invent proscribed occult books and new pantheon gods as well. These additions began to accumulate rapidly as the 1930s wore on. Clark Ashton Smith's "Ubbo-Sathla" brought in the sinister *Book of Eibon* and the oddly glowing stone of the sorcerer Zon Mezzamalach, just as Henry Kuttner's "The Salem Horror" featured the god Nyogtha and the witch Abigail Prinn. Kuttner's story, incidentally, is a sound Mythos tale but is almost wholly derivative, being modeled unabashedly on Lovecraft's "Dreams in the Witch-House."

"The Return of Hastur," written by August Derleth during the last year of Lovecraft's life, was not published until 1939. Introducing the god Hastur—which Derleth appropriated from Lovecraft, who got it from Robert Chambers, who had gotten it from Bierce—the story explains that Hastur is the half-brother of Cthulhu. It almost seems as if Derleth had been trying to write the ultimate or archetypal Mythos story in "The Return of Hastur," since it is set in Lovecraft's familiar mythical Massachusetts country, it drops the name of virtually every god and forbidden book contributed to the Mythos up to that time, and it even goes so far as to mention "The Call of Cthulhu" as having been written by Lovecraft.

Perhaps the most famous story associated with additions to Lovecraft's Mythos was that concerning Robert Bloch. While not all the additional Mythos stories were written during Lovecraft's life, Bloch's "The Shambler from the Stars" was, and the young Bloch, unwilling to rankle Lovecraft whom he greatly admired, wrote to Lovecraft asking his permission to use him as a character in "The Shambler." Furthermore, Bloch wanted to kill Lovecraft in the story. Lovecraft found this jest just to his liking, and he sent Bloch a quasi-legal document permitting Bloch to maim and murder him in the tale. The document was signed by Abdul Alhazred and a host of Lovecraft's monstrous gods. "The Shambler from the Stars" was published in 1934, and two years later Lovecraft's lighthearted means of revenge against Bloch saw print. This was "The Haunter of the Dark," in which one Robert Blake, a horror story writer from Wisconsin who is living at 66 College Street in Providence, is dispatched by "an avatar of Nyarlathotep."

To give some sense of how close Lovecraft was in spirit to other members of his literary circle, but how far away physically, it may be noted that the whole Lovecraft-Bloch interchange occurred by correspondence and that Bloch himself did not have occasion to visit the site of his own "death" and to see the Samuel Mumford house in Providence wherein he was "slain" until he attended the First World Fantasy Convention in Providence in 1975! And it is altogether fitting that during the convention, Bloch was presented with the first H. P. Lovecraft Life Award for his outstanding lifelong contributions to the field of fantasy and horror.

In the decade that followed Lovecraft's death, there was a great resurgence of interest in the work of the Providence dreamer. Whereas Mythos stories by HPL and the others had appeared only in the pages of *Weird Tales* and some other pulp publications, it was largely through the good offices of Derleth and fellow weird-fiction writer Donald Wandrei that Lovecraft was finally collected in book form. Derleth and Wandrei had formed a publishing enterprise known as Arkham House, named after Lovecraft's most famous fictive locale. Arkham House's primary function, in the beginning at any rate, was to publish the works of Lovecraft. In 1939 Arkham House brought out its first Lovecraft collection in a printing of a little over a thousand. This was *The Outsider and Others*, and it was the first time Lovecraft's fiction had ever been collected, although several of his stories had appeared previously in anthologies of weird fiction. This volume not only meant a wider exposure of Lovecraft's work, but it also signaled the beginning of the Sauk City, Wisconsin, publishing house that would bring out a dozen more Lovecraft books and would publish fiction and verse by J. Sheridan Le Fanu, M. P. Shiel, Basil Copper, Joseph Payne Brennan, Ramsey Campbell, Clark Ashton Smith, Lin Carter, Brian Lumley, and numerous other fantasists.

Later on, Derleth's publishing adjunct to Arkham House, Mycroft and Moran, would publish Derleth's own Solar Pons stories, those fine pastiches of the Sherlock Holmes adventures that finally won Derleth investiture in the Baker Street Irregulars of New York, his induction into that learned organization coming ironically in 1971, the year of his death. Even after Derleth's passing, however, Arkham House continued to publish weird fiction, and the house is still viable today.

But Derleth did not stay idle in terms of the HPL Mythos even while Arkham House was growing. In 1944 *Weird Tales* printed two Derleth Mythos stories, "The Dweller in Darkness" and "Beyond the Threshold." And he had also been preparing some of the first of what came to be called the Derleth-Lovecraft collaborations. Actually, what Derleth had done was to secure some of Lovecraft's rough notes and half-formed outlines for stories that were left unwritten upon Lovecraft's death. Working from his solid knowledge of Lovecraft's mythology and technique, Derleth proceeded to finish these stories. Finally, after they had appeared in pulp magazines or in other Arkham House collections, all sixteen of the Derleth-Lovecraft stories were brought together in the Arkham House volume entitled *The Watchers Out of Time and Others*, published in 1974.

During the period that the rise of Arkham House was bringing Lovecraft to a wider reading audience, interest in the Mythos he created continued to broaden. In 1951 Bloch, older now, turned again to the Mythos pastiche, producing "The Shadow from the Steeple" and "Notebook Found in a Deserted House," and these were printed in *Weird Tales*, which even at that late date still remained dedicated to the Lovecraftian story.

And an ever-widening circle of writers began to find Mythos stories lurking in their typewriters. One of the major forums for these works, since *Weird Tales* had expired in 1954, was *The Arkham Collector*, a quarterly magazine put out by Arkham House and devoted to Lovecraftiana. It was meant to be a replacement for a similar periodical, *The Arkham Sampler*, which ran for eight issues during 1948 and 1949 and which was the original place of publication for Lovecraft's "Dream-Quest of Unknown Kadath." *The Arkham Collector* existed for a total of ten issues from 1967 to 1971 and printed fiction, verse, and essays on Lovecraftian subjects by Lovecraft's former wife, Sonia, Joseph Payne Brennan, Lin Carter, L. Sprague de Camp, William Hope Hodgeson, Brian Lumley, Donald Wandrei, Wade Wellman, Robert Aikman, and Donald A. Wollheim among many others.

In the meantime, pastiches began to appear elsewhere. Brian Lumley wrote Mythos novels such as *The Burrowers Beneath, The Transition of Titus Crow,* and *Beneath the Moors*. The well-known critic, scholar, and author Colin Wilson utilized Mythos themes in his novels *The Outsider, The Mind Parasites,* and *The Philosopher's Stone*. In fact, Lovecraftian pastiches are appearing today in both the commercial press and privately published little magazines with such rapidity that bibliographers are hard-pressed to keep up with them.

Even so, however, Lovecraft's original tales of that grisly pantheon of monster-gods can brook no comparison with those that were added to the Mythos. While many of the Mythos additions are quite well written, it simply seems quite impossible for anyone to capture the general ambience of suffocating antiquity and decay that pervades the genuine article. That the Lovecraft inner circle spiraled outward from the seven writers of the 1930s to the scores of pastiches circulating through the bookstores and little magazines of today is a tribute not so much to those many writers caught by Lovecraft's spell as to the spell itself. It is a sign that while many may haunt the periphery of Lovecraft's occult vision, only one man saw it clearly enough to make it real.

This chapter synopsizes the plots of all of Lovecraft's significant fiction publications. The index, including both Lovecraft's juvenilia and his mature work, is presented alphabetically. Each entry consists of the story's title, the year (either precisely, or approximately when the exact year is not known) during which the story was composed, the place and date of its first publication, and a brief summary of the plot.

In addition, fourteen entries contain extended discussions of Lovecraft's geographical, biographical, and literary sources for the stories. It has been said frequently that for all the fantastic elements in HPL's fiction there is an amazing sense of reality. Lovecraft's talent for making fiction look like truth comes primarily from his use of real geographical settings and faithfully recounted historical fact as the backdrop against which his mythical dramas are enacted.

Since Lovecraft was a great antiquarian and a tireless researcher into New England's past, he had a vast storehouse of factual material upon which to draw in constructing his fiction. Also, his residing in New England, where historical societies and historical collections in university libraries are the rule rather than the exception, provided him readily with archival resources for his research.

2

The plots and sources of the stories

There is probably no error in saying that Lovecraft spent many more hours poring over the genealogical and historical collections of Brown University in Providence, the Essex Institute in Salem, and the Widener Library at Harvard than he did in actually writing fiction. But aside from studying at these major scholarly institutions, Lovecraft also devoted months to travel throughout New England, and during these journeys he visited the most remote villages as well as the largest cities. In the course of these trips, he carried on a campaign of acquiring great amounts of historical data that he later incorporated into his tales, particularly into his Mythos stories.

The result of this, that feeling of uneasiness that comes from recognizing truth in the midst of fiction, is just what Lovecraft wanted. While it is beyond the scope of this book to touch on every source in Lovecraft's work, it will become evident, through the examination of several major sources, how Lovecraft commingled the actual and the imaginary with such startling force.

"THE ALCHEMIST" (1908)
(*The United Amateur*, November 1916)

Ever since the thirteenth century when Count Henri de C— — ended the life of a wizard known as Michel Mauvais, a curse of early death has lain over the family of de C— —. It had been Michel Mauvais's son, Charles le Sorcier, who pronounced the original curse. The story line picks up in contemporary times with Antoine de C— — as the narrator. He learns of the curse and endeavors to take steps to protect himself from it.

One day, Antoine comes upon a bearded man wearing old-fashioned robes and a skullcap in an underground chamber on the de C— — estate. When the stranger attempts to murder Antoine, the secret of the ancient curse is revealed.

"ARTHUR JERMYN" (1920)
(*Weird Tales*, April 1924; appeared under the title "The White Ape")

Beginning with the eighteenth century African explorer Sir Wade Jermyn, there has been a seemingly hereditary madness and physical peculiarity about the Jermyn family. The tale of his ancestors' exploration of Africa and the bizarre story of a race of white apes presided over by a white ape goddess lead young Arthur Jermyn to investigate his family history.

"AT THE MOUNTAINS OF MADNESS" (1931)
(*Astounding Stories*, serialized February-April 1936)

This story, suggested to Lovecraft by Poe's "Narrative of A. Gordon Pym," is that of the Miskatonic University expedition to the Antarctic. But here, in this tale, there are frightful details of what that expedition discovered, details that did not find their way into the newspaper accounts.

The narrative proper gets under way with a subexpedition, led by Professor Lake, toward an Antarctic mountain range. It seems that Lake's party blunders upon some unknown life form, presumably in fossil form, after which the entire group perishes.

It is then up to the story's narrator, a professor of science at Miskatonic, and a young graduate student named Danforth to make a further investigation into the mountainous area. What the narrator and Danforth discover is a great plateau covered with gigantic obsidian stone structures—the ruins of a city peopled at one time by the so-called Old Ones (half-vegetable, half-animal, squidlike creatures with starfish heads). Through carvings on the walls of the city, the explorers learn of the Old Ones' history, of their descent from the stars, their wars with other alien species and of their tremendous fear of yet *another* mountain range beyond their own Plateau of Leng.

"THE BEAST IN THE CAVE" (1905)
(*The Vagrant*, June 1918)

Having become lost in Kentucky's Mammoth Cave, the narrator is about to give up when he hears the sound of approaching footsteps. When it becomes clear that he has not heard the sound of human footsteps and when the creature in the darkness seems ready to attack, the narrator grabs up a jagged piece of limestone and hurls it in the direction of the beast. Soon the narrator is found by a cave guide, and then the two of them start off in search of whatever it was that had seemed to press so close to the narrator in the darkness.

In this early Lovecraft story the narrator becomes "hopelessly lost in the vast and labyrinthine recesses of the Mammoth Cave." It is unlikely that at his young age Lovecraft had even been to Mammoth Cave in west-central Kentucky, but this is surely the setting for the story nevertheless. Proof for this exists in Lovecraft's referring to the cave's being on the Green River, as indeed the Kentucky cave is. But whether Lovecraft visited the cave with its three miles of commercial trails or simply read about it, he gives an accurate description of the "pleasant hills and dales of the beautiful world outside" as well as of the interior of the cave. He even mentions the "colony of consumptives" who took "their residence in this gigantic grotto to find health from the apparently salubrious air." Today guides in the cave will point out these so-called "consumptive huts" to the tourist, along with the apparatus that was used for the mining of nitrates in the cavern during the nineteenth century.

Mammoth Cave is just as mysterious a place as HPL depicted it as being, particularly owing to the display, in a glass case, of the well-preserved remains of an Indian who, while scraping gypsum from the walls, was trapped and killed by a collapsed stone ceiling. The body of "Lost John," as the Indian is referred to, was not discovered until 1935, many years after HPL wrote "The Beast in the Cave." Yet numerous other Indian skeletons were found there, the first in 1814. It was, perhaps, one of these strange relics that inspired Lovecraft to write his tale of the creature in Mammoth Cave.

"BEYOND THE WALL OF SLEEP" (1919)
(*Pine Cones*, October 1919)

During the winter of 1900-1901, a backwoods dweller in the Catskill Mountains is brought to an asylum after having committed a murder that apparently proceeded from his having visions of a fantastic world that lies beyond the corporeal. This world is populated by luminous beings, a race to which Slater, the murderer, believes he belongs. He is convinced that there is an enemy in this world that it is his duty to slay as an act of revenge.

Slater's ravings slowly begin to convince the narrator (who is employed at the asylum) that there is an element of truth in them. Acting on a theory that prompted him to construct an electronic device that permits the joining of two minds, the narrator proceeds to explore the intellect of Slater. But as the experiment begins, a voice comes to the narrator's mind proclaiming that Slater is dead and that his body has only been the vehicle for a wandering, luminous intelligence. A titanic battle that ranges across space and time is revealed, and its truth is borne out by an otherwise rather ordinary astronomical discovery.

"THE CALL OF CTHULHU" (1926)
(*Weird Tales*, February 1928)

One of Lovecraft's most complete and revelatory stories in terms of his Mythos, "The Call of Cthulhu" details the characteristics of the Cthulhu cult as it appears in various parts of the world, including the South Seas, Greenland, and the southern United States. This narrative is a complex one that deals with a peculiar madness that seems to attack sensitive persons on a certain date, the appearance of similar strange monolithic sculptures discovered at about the same time but in vastly different parts of the earth, and tales of a great legendary sea monster whose existence would not only be fantastic but would also portend evil on the earth of an absolutely unimaginable magnitude. It is the unfortunate lot of the story's narrator to be in a position to piece together all of this bizarre information and to be able to understand what it all means.

Cthulhu, the sea god of Lovecraft's extraterrestrial pantheon, rules the submarine deeps of R'lyeh, a city, according to its tradition, that will rise from the sea permitting its inhabitants to inherit the earth. In all probability Cthulhu is based on the Norwegian myth of the Kraken, a legendary monster thought to live under the waves of the northern seas. Lovecraft was well read in both world mythology and English literature, and although he might not have come directly in contact with the Norwegian myth, he could hardly have missed Alfred Lord Tennyson's poem "The Kraken":

Below the thunders of the upper deep;
Far, far beneath in the absymal sea,
His ancient, dreamless, uninvaded sleep
The Kraken sleepeth; faintest sunlights fell
About his shadowy sides: above him swell
Huge sponges of millennial growth and height;
And far away into the sickly light,
From many a wondrous grot and secret cell
Unnumber'd and enormous polypi
Winnow with giant arms the slumbering green.
There hath he lain for ages and will lie
Battening upon huge seaworms in his sleep,

Until the latter fire shall heat the deep;
Then once by man and angels to be seen,
In roaring he shall rise and on the surface die.

In "The Call of Cthulhu" are found the following lines from Lovecraft's magical grimoire the *Necronomicon: Ph'nglui mglw'nafh Cthulhu R'lyeh wgah'nagl fhgatn*. This is translated in the story as: "In his house at R'lyeh dead Cthulhu waits dreaming." Comparing these lines with those of Tennyson's poem, we find that both Cthulhu and the Kraken are marine beasts who sleep, the Kraken dreamlessly and Cthulhu dreaming. In both the poem and the story it is said that these creatures will rise up again in a hideous display of power. Although Cthulhu's mountaintop house at R'lyeh actually stands beneath the surface of the water, it is forced above the water line due to a seismic eruption similar to that in "The Kraken" ("the latter fire shall heat the deep"). Lovecraft also employed this device in his early short story "Dagon," wherein just such an eruption heaves up a submerged island on which roams the Dagon figure that forms one-third of the Dagon-Cthulhu-Deep Ones triad of undersea monsters.

"The Call of Cthulhu" is a story set in many parts of the world: New Orleans, the South Pacific, Oslo (hence the link with Norway and the Kraken myth), St. Louis. But the section that takes place in Lovecraft's own home city of Providence, Rhode Island, presents a feature of interest. This concerns Henry Anthony Wilcox, a young sculptor who, in a fevered dream, unaccountably carves an image of Cthulhu and dreams in the terrible language of the *Necronomicon*. Wilcox is presented to us as a student at the famous Rhode Island School of Design, Providence's renowned art school. His address is given as 7 Thomas Street in the "Fleur-de-Lys Building near that institution." This edifice in fact exists and can be seen today (see Figure 2). Thomas Street is on a short, steep hill that runs up to picturesque Benefit Street at its eastern end, and down to the Providence River to the west. Number 7 is a thin, high, and very dark half-timbered affair reminiscent of seventeenth-century England, with leaded, diamond-shaped windowpanes and decorated with odd paintings and reliefs on its façade. Lovecraft called it the Fleur-de-Lys Building because of the fleur-de-lys design that stands in relief over its doorway.

Wilcox is said to have had a falling out with the Providence Art Club, but Lovecraft does not mention in the story how very awkward this would be for Wilcox, since the Providence Art Club was and is located

Figure 2. Fleur-de-Lys Building, Providence, R.I. ''. . . the Fleur-de-Lys Building in Thomas Street, a hideous Victorian imitation of Seventeenth Century Breton architecture. . . .'' Photo by Philip A. Shreffler.

at 9 Thomas Street, just two doors away from Wilcox's house. The Art Club is lodged in the old Seril Dodge house, which was built in 1878. Seril Dodge and his brother Nehemiah had become prominent citizens of Providence when they perfected a gold-plating process leading to that town's great industry of making costume jewelry, itself ironically antithetical to the Art Club that would one day take over the Dodge house.

"THE CASE OF CHARLES DEXTER WARD" (1927-1928)
(*Weird Tales*, May and July 1941)

One of Lovecraft's most powerful stories, this concerns young Charles Ward, a student in Providence, Rhode Island, who becomes involved in an investigation of a particular ancestor of his, one Joseph Curwin who had fled Salem, Massachusetts, at the time of the 1692 witch hysteria that had originated at Danvers (then Salem Village). As a result of the discovery of a number of old documents, Ward comes to learn that Curwin was indeed a wizard who was associated with several other powerful magicians in Puritan Massachusetts, including Simon Orne and Edward Hutchinson.

Ward finds out that Curwin, Orne, and Hutchinson were practicing magic not in the rather traditional and conventional manner assumed by the Calvinistic Puritan prosecutors but, on a greater scale, with the intention of unlocking forbidden secrets from beyond time and space. This was to be effected through a kind of worldwide necromantic conspiracy that depended upon the accumulated magical wisdom of history's greatest practitioners of the black arts. Slowly, a spell of morbid interest in Curwin's grand design begins to creep over Charles Dexter Ward, and that spell grows to what must eventually be a destructive level.

It was certainly Lovecraft's living in Providence that occasioned a long digression at the beginning of "The Case of Charles Dexter Ward" in order that the author might take the reader on a loving sightseeing tour of the city. The first point of interest on the tour is Ward's own birthplace and family home, "a great Georgian mansion atop the well nigh precipitous hill that rises just east of the river" and which has "a double-bayed brick façade." The house that Lovecraft had in mind here is the Halsey Mansion at 140 Prospect Street on College Hill, four blocks above the Providence River. The Halsey Mansion is one of the most impressive of Prospect Street's great old houses. It is an immense two-storied brick building that does feature a convex bay on either side of the central doorway, the bays extending from foundations to roof. The imposing aspect of the Halsey Mansion, created partly by the massive bays, is augmented by the fact that the back wings of the house reach out toward the downward slope of College Hill and, as in the story, command a view of the Providence River (see Figure 3).

"The little white farmhouse of two hundred years before" that Lovecraft describes as standing near the Ward house exists in Providence as well, just across the street and about a half-block south of the Halsey Mansion. This cottage was one of the original houses in the area and was built before 1775.

"Prospect Terrace" or Prospect Park on Congdon Street, a block below Prospect, where Ward's nurse used to "chat with policemen," was also one of Lovecraft's own favorite resting places in Providence. Today, Prospect Park is much as it was in Lovecraft's day, a pleasant little park, about the size of a house lot, where trees, park benches, and a monument dedicated to Roger Williams all overlook metropolitan Providence to the west. The place is now often frequented by students from nearby Brown University.

One of the oldest and most pleasant avenues in Providence is Benefit Street, characterized by HPL as having "long lines of pre-Revolutionary homes with their great central chimneys and classic portals. On the eastern side they were set high over basements with railed double flights of stone steps. . . ." It is also on Benefit Street that one will find "The Shunned House" (q.v.), and today almost all of those old houses have been restored to their original beauty.

Another landmark mentioned by Lovecraft that still stands is the Cathedral of St. John (1772), a great Gothic structure of stone. In its adjacent graveyard Lovecraft once told a young lady such fearful ghost stories that she fled the place in terror.

As the story of Ward progresses, we learn that the villain of the tale is a wizard and necromancer named Joseph Curwin who fled Salem, Massachusetts, during the witchcraft hysteria of 1692 for the more tolerant and benevolent atmosphere of Rhode Island. There was, in fact, a family named Curwin in Salem at that time (spelled variously Corwin and Carwin but always pronounced Curwin). A certain George Corwin was the sheriff of Essex County during the trials, but there was one particular Curwin who was surely the equal of Joseph Curwin in his evil and who was also probably Lovecraft's model for the sinister

Figure 3. The Halsey Mansion, Providence, R. I. ". . . a great Georgian mansion . . . [with a] double-bayed brick facade . . . " Photo by Philip A. Shreffler.

wizard. He was Judge Jonathan Corwin, the local magistrate who was Judge John Hathorne's right-hand man during the preliminary hearings in the witchcraft incident.

When the trials themselves got under way, the three presiding judges were Hathorne, Samuel Sewell, and William Stoughton. But in the preliminary hearings there were only Hathorne and Corwin. It is altogether possible that had Hathorne been less insistent, the witch hysteria might have died early. But Hathorne was out to find witches, come what may, and Jonathan Corwin proved to be an all-too-willing accomplice in the insanity. Actually, Corwin was little more than a yes man extracting from the defendants what Hathorne wanted to hear and supporting Hathorne by cosigning indictments with him. If Hathorne's was the more monstrous evil, Corwin's was the most insidious because of his refusal to see Hathorne for what he was. It is said that more than 200 accused witches were brought to Corwin's own home for examination. It is therefore not difficult to see why Lovecraft might have chosen him for the image of Joseph Curwin.

In "Charles Dexter Ward," Joseph Curwin's compatriot in the necromantic scheme is a Simon Orne, also of Salem and also a refugee from the Court of Oyer and Terminer. Lovecraft had done his homework here as well, since the Orne family is also well known in Salem history, but not for any involvement in the witchcraft business. A map of Salem in 1700 shows several plots of land on Town House Street (now Washington Street) as belonging to the Ornes. But of signal interest to "Charles Dexter Ward" is the fact that the *Pedigree of the Hornes or Ornes of Salem, Massachusetts*, in the Essex Institute at Salem lists one Simon Orne as having been born on January 11, 1679 or 1680, grown up to be a weaver, and removed to Newport, Rhode Island, by 1711, just as Joseph Curwin had moved to Providence in HPL's story.

None of this, of course, is coincidence, for Lovecraft spent many, many hours in the Essex Institute researching genealogy, land grants, and similar matters. (An ephemeral note here might include the fact that one of the oldest houses of Salem, now owned by the Essex Institute, is the 1684 John Ward house, although it has always been assumed that Lovecraft derived the Ward name from the second part of How*ard*, his own first name.)

One of the more perplexing historical problems in "Charles Dexter Ward" is the notable group of vigilantes that organizes to end Joseph Curwin's career. This group includes Stephen Hopkins, a former governor of Rhode Island, and his brother Esah; Moses Brown, who endowed Brown University, and his brother John; and Captain James Whipple. What Lovecraft did here was to make fictional use of the real company of colonial vigilantes that was responsible on June 10, 1772, for burning the British revenue cutter *Gaspee* in Rhode Island's Narragansett Bay, thereby defying the tax-levying power of King George III. This is just one more in a long series of examples of HPL's ability to make the real fictional and the fictional real.

"THE CATS OF ULTHAR" (1920)
(*The Tryout*, November 1920)

The law in Ulthar is that no man may kill a cat. Before this law was passed, an old couple living in a dark cottage in Ulthar would destroy every cat they encountered.

One day, a caravan passes through Ulthar, and in the train is a young boy named Menes. When Menes's pet kitten disappears, and the boy hears word of the cruel behavior of the old couple, he performs what seems to be a rite of conjuration. That night, all the cats in Ulthar disappear, returning the next morning. And then it is discovered that the old couple of the cottage have vanished as well.

"CELEPHAIS" (1920)
(*The Rainbow*, May 1922)

Finding life in modern London ugly and tedious, the hero of this vignette creates a world called Celephais, which exists only in his dreams. Taking the name Kuranes in his dream world, the hero, having seen Celephais several times, soon finds himself unable to locate the fabulous place during the hours of sleep.

When normal sleep will not produce the vision, Kuranes turns to hashish in order to provoke the imaginary creation of Celephais. At length, a group of knights comes for Kuranes and leads him from London, through Surrey, and to the coast. The party travels through space and time until it reaches Celephais, where Kuranes is crowned as king and installed as god and creator.

This story is significant for its mention of the Plateau of Leng (prominent in the Mythos stories) and for locating the village of Innsmouth on the English coast (a town later located by Lovecraft in

Massachusetts and used as the setting for "The Shadow over Innsmouth").

"THE COLOUR OUT OF SPACE" (1927)
(*Amazing Stories*, September 1927)

It is to the farm of Nahum Gardner, nestled in the wild hills west of Arkham, that the color out of space comes, bringing with it madness and death. The terror at Gardner's farm began in the 1880s with the crashing of a meteorite, the like of which scientists from Miskatonic University had never before seen.

But the effects of the thing from space were odder still than the object itself. The flora and fauna of the area in which the meteorite landed began to behave monstrously and were characterized by a queer luminosity. Gardner's crops yielded nothing of use, and slowly every living thing on the farm simply began to waste away.

The enormous proportions of the evil involved with the phenomena do not, however, become apparent until members of Gardner's family begin to fall into madness, while the land surrounding his house decays into a "blasted heath."

"COOL AIR" (1926)
(*Tales of Magic and Mystery*, March 1928)

The narrator explains that his intense loathing of cool air is the result of his having taken rooms in an old brownstone house on New York's Fourteenth Street. For it is there that he meets the mysterious Spanish physician Dr. Muñoz. Muñoz, an aristocrat of obvious taste and breeding, has, it seems, contracted a disease that requires him to live in temperatures well below sixty degrees. To this end, he keeps a refrigeration unit in his rooms. As his condition deteriorates, Muñoz constantly seeks to lower the temperature. Strange as all this is, it is not half as strange as what happens on the day Muñoz's cooling unit breaks down altogether.

"DAGON" (1917)
(*The Vagrant*, November 1919)

The narrator, at the edge of madness, recounts how, during World War I, he is captured in the Pacific Ocean by a German raider from which he escapes in an open boat. While the narrator is unconscious, the boat is grounded on a slimy land mass that has heaved up from the ocean bottom. Exploring the island brings about the discovery of an ancient monolith inscribed with images of huge fish-men. But what comes to worship at the immense stone is the island's most terrible secret.

"THE DOOM THAT CAME TO SARNATH" (1919)
(*Scot*, June 1920)

In the land of Mnar once existed the city of Ib, inhabited by an unpleasant aquatic or reptilian folk who worshiped Bokrug, "the great water-lizard," to whom they had erected a sea-green idol. When men come to Mnar and establish the magnificent city of Sarnath, they come to hate the creatures of Ib and wage genocidal warfare against them. They slaughter the population and carry the idol of Bokrug back to Sarnath in triumph.

However, the night after the idol is brought to Sarnath, its keeper-priest is found dead and the idol gone. Strange lights are seen coming from the lake where the bodies of the Ib people had been thrown by their conquerers.

Over the next thousand years, Sarnath prospers and becomes the most splendid city of the earth. But on the thousandth anniversary of the destruction of Ib, lights are again seen in the lake, and Sarnath, in the midst of celebration, is confronted by its age-old enemy.

"THE DREAM-QUEST OF UNKNOWN KADATH" (1926)
(*The Arkham Sampler*, serialized Winter-Autumn 1948)

In this, one of the longest of Lovecraft's fictive works, it is Randolph Carter who slips off into the world of dreams in search for the ultimate city of Kadath, the dwelling place of the Great Old Ones in "the cold waste." A picaresque series of events of the swords and sorcery variety leads Carter onward toward his goal. Along the way, he meets such beasts and monsters as the ghasts, the ghouls, the night-gaunts, the Gugs, and a host of others, including the terrific Nyarlathotep, in adventures that take him to the moon in a black galley and to the forbidden Plateau of Leng.

"THE DREAMS IN THE WITCH-HOUSE" (1932)
(*Weird Tales*, July 1933)

In the New England hamlet of Arkham, Walter Gilman, a student at Miskatonic University, takes a room in the garret of a reputedly haunted house once inhabited by Keziah Mason, a witch condemned in the hysteria of 1692. Legend has it that Keziah had drawn secret devices on the wall of her cell and had vanished just before the sentence pronounced upon her by Judge John Hathorne could be executed.

The Witch-House is well suited for Gilman, who is engaged in the study of both non-Euclidean physics as well as certain forms of ancient magical lore. Gradually, some of the peculiar features of architectural geometry in the house, along with a series of bizarre occurrences, begin to connect themselves with old Keziah.

Gilman has nightmares in which not only the old witch appears but also the form of her "familiar," Brown Jenkin, an abnormal ratlike creature with tiny human hands instead of feet and a bearded human face. These creatures accompany Gilman, in his dreams, into a sort of parallel dimension that seems to lie beyond an oddly angled wall in Gilman's garret room.

As Gilman assembles the facts about his weird experiences, everything seems to point, however incredible it seems, to there being inexplicable elements of truth in the Arkham legends of Black Masses on May Eve involving human sacrifice, the appearance of the fabled Black Man of the witches, and the continued existence of Keziah Mason and Brown Jenkin.

This tale, another of Lovecraft's strange blends of pure fantasy and otherdimensional fiction, is set against the backdrop of the "legend-haunted city of Arkham, with its clustering gambrel roofs that sway and sag over attics where witches hid. . . ." Since HPL modeled Arkham on Salem, Massachusetts, one may read Salem for Arkham, and by the Witch-House in Arkham we understand Lovecraft to mean the Witch-House in Salem. Indeed, the Witch-House in Salem was called by that name in Lovecraft's day just as it was through the nineteenth century.

A peculiar feature of the Gilman-Mason room in the Witch-House is the fact that the north wall slants "perceptibly' inward from the outer to the inner end, while the low ceiling slanted gently downward in the same direction." It is what Gilman finds beyond this oddly angled wall that is the cause of his greatest terror.

The Witch-House in Salem upon which Lovecraft modeled Arkham's house of the same name was originally the home of Judge Jonathan Corwin, the assistant magistrate to Judge Hathorne in the preliminary hearings of the Court of Oyer and Terminer at Salem in 1692. It was through this house that over 200 men and women accused of witchcraft passed as Judges Hathorne and Corwin took depositions for use in the celebrated Salem witchcraft trials.

The house now stands at the corner of Essex and North streets in Salem, having been moved several yards south of its original location (see Figure 4). Judge Corwin's house was built in 1675 and by the nineteenth century had become quite a tourist attraction, even to the present day. By the late 1800s, the Witch-House had been virtually swallowed up by the surrounding buildings, so much so as to have an apothecary shop attached to its southeast front facade. This is the way Lovecraft saw the Witch-House in the 1920s and 1930s, and it was not until well into the twentieth century that the apothecary shop was torn down, the house moved to its present prominent position, and the whole building restored to its original condition.

Today, a tour guide ushers visitors through the house, which is basically a rectangle with a single room on either side of an entry hall and staircase, both downstairs and up. The ground-floor rooms are set up as a seventeenth-century parlor and dining room, while the two upstairs rooms are bedrooms, all four rooms displaying the massive, dark fireplaces and heavy timbers typical of the period. It was in the western room on the second floor that Judge Corwin held his famous hearings, although the innocuous furnishings there do not betray much of a sense of horror.

A part of the house, however, that the tourist may not visit is reached by unlocking one of the two wooden doors leading to the attic (there is one such door in each of the second-floor rooms). Passing through either of these doors one finds himself in a cramped passage where a short flight of steep, rough-hewn steps take him through a trap door to the attic. Climbing through the trap door, one must step gingerly round the central fireplace chimney, which is at the head of the steps, and ease himself across the sagging planks of the attic floor.

Initially, the attic room of the Witch-House where Keziah supposedly hid herself is disappointing. It is completely unfinished, with no room divisions at all. Clutter and rubbish litter the corners, and the floor boards seem, frankly, unsafe. But then one will notice a peculiar architectural feature. The south wall (not the north as HPL stated)

Figure 4. The Witch House, Salem, Mass. "... it was this house ... which had likewise harbored old Kesiah Mason, whose flight from the Salem Gaol at the last no one was ever able to explain." Photo by Philip A. Shreffler.

slants inward at a strange angle, with the bottom against the outside wall of the house and the top sloping inward several feet away from the outside wall. There are gaps in this sloping wall, where the windows are located, and at these points one can peer around into the triangular space between the inner and outer walls. Immediately, one thinks of the similar feature in Gilman's room.

Actually, the reason for this is that the inner wall follows the shape of the roof, and the two spaces near the windows (where there are gaps) are outcroppings accounted for by two exterior gables. One may look into the space between the two walls near the windows simply because the gables have not been finished on the inside. Nevertheless, for a bewitching moment, one has the impression of having glimpsed the mysteries of Keziah's haunted Witch-House in old Arkham.

"THE DUNWICH HORROR" (1928)
(*Weird Tales*, April 1929)

The Whateleys of Dunwich, Massachusetts, had always been a strange family given to secrets that the locals considered supernatural. But it is with the birth and maturing of Wilbur Whateley that horror comes to Dunwich. Wilbur's chief interest is in the feared magical grimoire, the *Necronomicon*, a copy of which he seeks to obtain at any cost. This book contains rituals that Wilbur is particularly anxious to perform among the ancient stone ruins of the Devil's Hop-Yard atop Sentinel Hill, which stands near the Whateley farmstead.

The only man who seems capable of putting a stop to the hideous practices of the Whateleys is Dr. Henry Armitage of Miskatonic University at Arkham, Massachusetts. His putting the *Necronomicon* under lock and key in the university library was probably one of the most intelligent things he ever did, since that simple action brought to light the terrible nature of what had taken place at Dunwich and of what was about to take place.

One of the most fascinating yet troublesome aspects of "The Dunwich Horror," completed during 1928, is the mystery concerning just which geographical locations and what phenomena Lovecraft synthesized in his invention of the Dunwich, Massachusetts, area. According to Lovecraft himself, Dunwich corresponds to the hilly region around Wilbraham, Hampden, and Monson, in Massachusetts, just to the southeast of Springfield. And it seems to be a well-known fact among several literary scholars in Wilbraham that Lovecraft visited Edith Miniter, a novelist and amateur journalist who lived in that town. However, in fictionalizing the Wilbraham area, Lovecraft relocated Dunwich in "north central Massachusetts," which would seem to suggest a setting farther north, perhaps in the vicinity of what is now the Quabbin Reservoir. Furthermore, there are other suggestions in "The Dunwich Horror" that Lovecraft ranged as far north as southern New Hampshire and as far south as eastern Connecticut in gathering the features of setting for the story.

The traveler in the Wilbraham area surely will notice, as the story states, that "the ground gets higher, and the brier-bordered stone walls press closer and closer against the . . . curving road." Lovecraft is completely faithful to the topographical features, especially in describing the summits of the "mountains in view above the deep woods" as very much "too rounded and symmetrical to give a sense of comfort and naturalness." To use one of Lovecraft's favorite words, it is a truly "eldritch" experience to see these uncannily rounded hills rising up into the gray mist on a rainy afternoon.

Of the three towns mentioned (Wilbraham, Hampden, and Monson), it is perhaps Monson that most closely fits the description of Dunwich, "a small village huddled between the stream and the verticle slope of Round Mountain." Monson is nestled in between a massive round hill and a tributary of the Quaboag River and is, of the three towns, the quaintest in appearance (see Figure 5).

It is at this point, though, that the Wilbraham area ceases to resemble the setting of the story, and at which Lovecraft began importing characteristics from other locales to use in his tale. We know this because nowhere near Wilbraham or Monson are the hills "crowned" with "queer circles of tall stone pillars" as are most of the hills around Dunwich—in particular Sentinel Hill on the property of Old Whateley. Then how did Lovecraft invent Sentinel Hill with its curious Stonehenge-like circle of stones and "sizable table-like" altar that combine to form what he called the Devil's Hop-Yard?

First, Lovecraft's locating Dunwich in "north central Massachusetts" makes sense here, since there actually are examples of strange stone structures and odd rock carvings across the top of the state, approximately from the area of Shutesbury, Massachusetts (across the Connecticut River from which is the town of Whately), east to North Salem, New Hampshire, just above Lowell. Most such structures are small stone huts that have come to be called "beehives," and there are

Figure 5. Countryside Near Monson, Mass. "The summits [of the hills around Dunwich] are too rounded and symmetrical to give a sense of comfort and naturalness. . . ." Photo by Philip A Shreffler.

also some rock-lined tunnels as well as certain carvings in stone that seem to defy identification. Theories as to what artisans were responsible for these New England "megaliths" range from the predictable (colonists or Indians) through the remarkable (prehistoric visitors from Malta, tenth-century Irish monks, eleventh-century Vikings, fourteenth-century Scots) to the idiotic (extraterrestrials). But the structures are there all the same.

The most impressive of these sites is that at Mystery Hill (North Salem), New Hampshire, which Lovecraft visited with his friend H. Warner Munn. Here, within a half-acre plot, is a concentration of stone structures complete enough to look like a Stone Age village, with wells, small stone hovels, stones that seem to measure astronomical movements, walls, and so on. This commercial site's most popular artifact is the huge six-by-eight-foot slab called the sacrificial altar table (see Figure 6). The massive platform, which suggests the stone table of old Whateley's Devil's Hop-Yard, is deeply grooved around the outside with a runoff trough—ostensibly a blood gutter to drain the table after an animal sacrifice. However, there is another such stone in the Farm Museum at Hadley, Massachusetts, which the guide staunchly maintains is a seventeenth-century cider press base found in the woods "up near Goshen" (see Figure 7).

Most reputable scholars now tend to believe that the North Salem site was probably the work of a colonist named Pattee, who owned the land, although it is possible that Pattee built up many of the structures on top of some genuine Indian ruins. At any rate, Lovecraft apparently modified these structures to take on more of a Stonehenge-like appearance, appropriated the cider press base as a sacrificial altar table, and moved the whole works in his imagination to the oddly rounded hills of Wilbraham.

But this does not complete the story. Lovecraft also seems to have used another phenomenon. In "The Dunwich Horror" when the Whateleys perform their May Eve and All Hallows' Eve rites, the doings are accompanied by thunderlike explosions in the sky. There are at least two accounts of something similar happening in the days of the Puritans. Strange thunderous boomings that the Puritans usually attributed to the devil occurred for years at Nonanoicus Pond near the Massachusetts-Vermont border, and at Moodus, Connecticut, where the noises were reported as recently as 1970. These came to be called the Nonanoicus noises and the Moodus noises respectively, and they terrified people thereabouts, especially since no cause could be found.

Figure 6. "Sacrificial Altar Stone," North Salem, N.H. "... the top of Sentinel Hill where the old table-like stone stands amidst its tumulus of ancient bones." Photo by Philip A. Shreffler.

Figure 7. "Cider Press Base," Hadley, Mass. Photo by Philip A. Shreffler.

Lovecraft surely knew of, and used, particularly the Moodus noises in "The Dunwich Horror" because only about ten miles from Moodus, and near the town of East Haddam, Connecticut, may be found what is still known as the Devil's Hop-Yard (see Figure 8). Located in the center of the eighty-acre Devil's Hop-Yard State Park is a waterfall called Chapman's Falls. At the head of the falls are some rocks that the natural water action has hollowed out into large cauldron shapes. Legend has it that the witches of East Haddam convened there to brew potions in the bowl-shaped rocks, while the devil himself presided over the spectacle while playing a violin. Here, then, is the source of HPL's Devil's Hop-Yard on Dunwich's Sentinel Hill.

It is interesting to note that in reconstructing the sources for "The Dunwich Horror" we have moved from Wilbraham, Massachusetts, up to Shutesbury, across to North Salem, New Hampshire, and back down to East Haddam, Connecticut, only about a hundred miles from Lovecraft's own Providence.

"THE EVIL CLERGYMAN" (1937)
(*Weird Tales*, April 1939; appeared under the title "The Wicked Clergyman")

Here is a weird tale that breaks literary convention by dint of its having virtually no exposition to set up the conditions of the plot. The narrator simply finds himself in a strange house somewhere near London. Through the use of a sort of ray projector that he finds in his pocket, he summons the forms of a group of clergymen, dressed as Anglicans, but clearly the members of a secret magical cult. Prominent among them is a young, clean-shaven man who menaces the narrator to the point where the narrator turns his ray projector on his presumed attacker. The results are terrible but, as is pointed out, not necessarily fatal.

"THE FESTIVAL" (1923)
(*Weird Tales*, January 1925)

In this story the narrator is summoned to the ancient colonial-period village of Kingsport, Massachusetts, to take part in Yule rites that are older than mankind. The ritual, brought to New England in the 1600s by the narrator's ancestors, begins with a procession from a house in Green Lane to the old church on Central Hill. Into the catacombs be-

Figure 8. The Devil's Hop-yard, East Haddam, Conn. ". . the Devil's Hop-Yard—a bleak, blasted hillside where no tree, shrub or blade of grass will grow." Photo by Philip A Shreffler.

neath the church streams the procession, but what the narrator confronts there causes him to regret ever having been a part of the festival.

Upon entering Marblehead, Massachusetts (see Figure 9), the coastal town that Lovecraft renamed Kingsport, from the direction of Salem (Arkham), one is struck by how very true are the first impressions of HPL's narrator in "The Festival," who approaches the town from the same direction:

beyond the hill's crest I saw . . . Kingsport with its ancient vanes and steeples, ridgepoles and chimney-pots, wharves and small bridges, willow trees and graveyards; endless labryinths of steep, narrow, crooked streets, and dizzy church-crowned central peak that time durst not touch; ceaseless mazes of colonial houses piled and scattered at all angles and levels like a child's disordered blocks. . . .

Although it is not difficult to recognize Marblehead in this description, it is not so easy to identify the two buildings in Lovecraft's Kingsport that are specifically mentioned in the story. This is because Lovecraft fictionalized Marblehead's street names and the names of certain landmarks. Nevertheless, it is possible to locate both the house to which the narrator goes upon his arrival in Kingsport, as well as the church in which the sinister Yule rites are held (see Figure 10).

To find the home of the narrator's people, it is necessary to approach Marblehead (Kingsport) from the direction of Salem (Arkham) by progressing down "Back Street." In contemporary Marblehead there is no Back Street; however, street signs inform the traveler that the present Elm Street was once known as Back Street.

One must then proceed along Back Street until one reaches "Circle Court" and from there progress "to where Green Lane leads off behind the Market House." This is confusing because Circle Court, Green Lane, and the Market House also do not exist under those names. However, moving east along Elm Street will lead one to where Elm, Pond, Mugford, and Green Streets all meet to form a sort of open traffic circle or rotary, which we may take to be HPL's fictional Circle Court. We next need to locate Lovecraft's Market House. Here Lovecraft can only be referring to the 1727 Town House, the first civil government building in Marblehead and the site of open-air markets in the eighteenth and nineteenth centuries.

Now there remains only to find the street called Green Lane, which

Figure 9. Marblehead, Mass. ". . . I saw Kingsport . . . with its . . . endless labyrinths of steep, narrow, crooked streets, and . . . ceaseless mazes of colonial houses piled and scattered at all angles and levels like a child's disordered blocks. . . ." Photo courtesy of The Essex Institute, Salem, Mass.

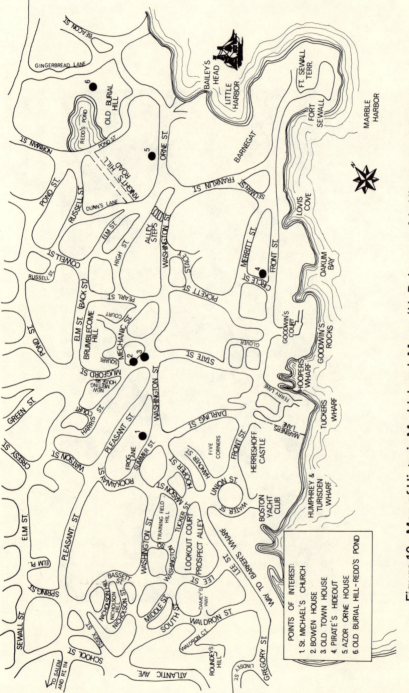

Figure 10.   Map of Historic Marblehead, Mass. (H. P. Lovecraft's Kingsport, Mass.)

must be a street veering off behind the Town House and running up toward Circle Court. And Mugford Street is our only choice (and the logical one, since it literally forms an extension of Green Street).

According to the tale, the house for which the narrator looks is the "seventh house on the left in Green Lane, with an ancient peaked roof and jutting second story, all built before 1650." The only house on Mugford Street (and indeed one of the few in Marblehead) with a jutting or garrisoned second story is actually the tenth house on the left going southeast from Circle Court. This is the Bowen House at 1 Mugford Street, built in 1695 by William Waters (see Figure 11). Not only does the Bowen House exhibit the prominent garrisoned second story, but it also possesses "the low stone doorstep" mentioned in the tale.

The church in which the evil rituals of Kingsport are held is rather a simpler matter. It must be a church with "a churchyard with spectral shafts" and must have a burial crypt underneath the nave. St. Michael's Episcopal Church on Summer Street, erected in 1714, does indeed have such a cemetery on its east side (see Figure 12).

Just where Lovecraft found information regarding the existence of a crypt under the church is unknown. Either he was psychic or he managed to locate satisfactory evidence of the crypt's existence in some presently unremembered source. In fact, St. Michael's has no "trap-door . . . just before the pulpit" as the story suggests. However, the church's official historian, Robert Howie, states that such a crypt does indeed exist beneath the building.

Until recently, Howie's conviction about the crypt was based only on documentary evidence (diaries, town histories, and so on) indicating that burials were made underneath the church, and on a document stating that during a renovation project in the early 1920s a number of skeletons were exhumed and reinterred in the cemetery. It was in 1923, at about the time this news was current, that Lovecraft wrote "The Festival," and this information might have provided him with a rudimentary source upon which he elaborated.

But it was not until 1976 that Lovecraft's seemingly fanciful tale of a crypt "just before the pulpit" was proven to be accurate. Surprisingly, though, the newly discovered crypt is not located under the present altar, but under an older, hidden altar. In a letter to me dated December 1, 1976, Howie wrote:

Figure 11. The Bowen House, Marblehead, Mass. ". . . the seventh house on the left in Green Lane, with an ancient peaked roof and jutting second story . . ." Photo by Philip A. Shreffler.

Figure 12. St. Michael's Episcopal Church, Marblehead, Mass. "There was an open space around the church; partly a churchyard with spectral shafts, and partly a half-paved square. . . ." Photo courtesy of The Essex Institute, Salem, Mass.

If there was any doubt in the past as to the existence of a crypt beneath this church, they can be laid to rest now. . . . We have overwhelming evidence that people were buried beneath St. Michael's. . . . We have, in fact, begun excavating beneath the church. . . . The original entrance was discovered when I broke down a brick retaining wall put up over a hundred years ago. It is located in the south-east corner of the church about 10 feet from the existing front entrance which you may recall from your visit here. This opening in the foundation wall led underneath to the altar which was on the east side of the church. (The altar was moved to the north in 1832 and the entire insides of the church transformed.) It was probably beneath the original altar that a few people were buried. This part of the project will begin this week. Already we have excavated other areas and completed a surface survey which produced numerous tibia, scapula and even a scalp with hair still intact. Lovecraft would have loved it!

"FROM BEYOND" (1920)
(*The Fantasy Fan*, June 1934)

Crawford Tillinghast, a resident of East Providence, Rhode Island, has developed electrical machinery that permits glimpses into a parallel world that exists contiguous to our own but in another dimension. Incredible as it sounds, this theory is demonstrated by Tillinghast for the story's narrator. However, Tillinghast has become power crazed by his discovery and takes a perverse pleasure in *what* he has seen in the parallel world and in the manner in which his servants have disappeared.

This early story, perhaps, reflects the theme of a monstrous parallel dimension that was used later by Lovecraft in the Mythos stories.

"THE HAUNTER OF THE DARK" (1935)
(*Weird Tales*, December 1936)

Robert Blake, a Wisconsin author of horror stories, takes up residence in Providence, Rhode Island, and while there becomes fascinated by the ancient Free-Will Baptist Church on Federal Hill. Drawn to explore the abandoned Gothic structure, he discovers therein implications that the place has been used as the site of blasphemous magical ceremonies associated with the worship of that pantheon of gods that includes Yog-Sothoth, Azathoth, and Nyarlathotep. It is Blake's blundering upon this secret that seems to stir into a parody of life a certain vague creature that inhabits only regions of total darkness.

The Italians of the Federal Hill area, cowed into superstitious terror, call on a priest to attempt an exorcism, but, as revealed by Blake's diary, the writer of horror stories knows a truth about the old church that places it beyond the power of any priest.

Just beneath the title of "The Haunter of the Dark," one will notice that Lovecraft jotted in "Dedicated to Robert Bloch." In the earlier days of *Weird Tales* young Bloch found HPL to be an encouraging literary mentor. Bloch, usually best known for his authorship of *Psycho*, was living in Milwaukee at the time of his correspondence with Lovecraft and in 1935 decided to write a short story in which a character modeled on Lovecraft was hideously dispatched. The story was called "The Shambler from the Stars," and Bloch had secured HPL's light-hearted permission to annihilate fictionally the Providence writer.

The following year, Lovecraft published "The Haunter of the Dark" in *Weird Tales*, the story being HPL's friendly retaliation against Bloch. It is obvious that the fictional Blake of the tale is actually the oftentimes nonfictional Bloch.

The plot of the story involves Blake's curiosity about a massive old church whose bulk looms up on Providence's Federal Hill. The church, Blake comes to discover, is actually the headquarters of a bizarre ritual cult, and its steeple is the lair of a huge, largely undefined monster that, to poor Blake's peril, is confined to the tower only during the daylight hours.

Once again, Lovecraft employed the actual architectural features of Providence in his fiction. Although the church in the story is called the Free-Will Baptist Church, it was patterned after St. John's Roman Catholic Church located on Atwells Avenue about four blocks west of Interstate 95 (see Figure 13). As one looks west from College Hill at sunset, one sees, as does Blake, "the great tower and tapering steeple [looming] blackly against the flaming sky." Unfortunately, today the view is obscured a bit by a new hotel and a high-rise apartment building that add nothing to Providence's antique skyline.

Lovecraft describes the house in which Blake has taken rooms on the upper floor as

a venerable dwelling in a grassy court off College Street — on the crest of the great eastward hill near the Brown University campus and behind the marble

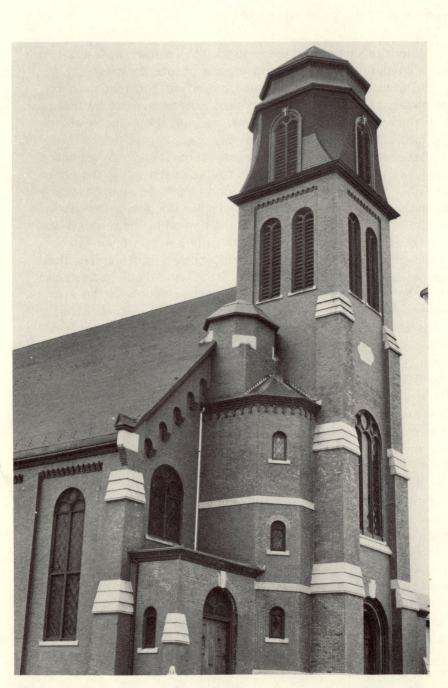

Figure 13. St. John's Roman Catholic Church, Providence, R.I. "... at sunset the great tower and tapering steeple loomed blackly against the flaming sky...." Photo by Philip A. Shreffler.

John Hay Library. . . . The square Georgian house had a monitor roof, classic doorway with fan carving, small-paned windows, and all the other earmarks of early Nineteenth Century workmanship.

This house is described with such loving attention to detail because it was not only Blake's residence but Lovecraft's own as well. What is being pictured here is the Samuel B. Mumford house, built in 1825, the edifice to which Lovecraft moved in 1933 and which was his last home. The Mumford-Lovecraft house originally stood at 66 College Street, as it does in the story, but has now been moved to 65 Prospect Street to make way for the enormous concrete structure of the Brown University Art Building (see Figure 14).

"HE" (1925)
(*Weird Tales*, September 1926)

Out for a nocturnal ramble in search of the architectural antiquities of Greenwich Village, the narrator encounters a stranger who is muffled in an overcoat and soft hat. The stranger, too, professes an interest in the antiquarian and offers to usher the narrator on a unique tour. The two make their way through the labyrinthine streets until they find themselves within a great house that was built before Greenwich ever existed. Here, removing his hat and coat, the stranger reveals himself as an apparent eccentric garbed in eighteenth-century clothing.

In the tale that the stranger unfolds, he is characterized as a magician possessed of certain fantastic abilities ostensibly learned from his ancestors. But his execution of a particular conjuration, along with the *effects* of that conjuration, prove him to be other than what he says he is and result in what is altogether terrifying.

"HERBERT WEST—REANIMATOR" (1921-1922)
(*Home Brew*, serialized February-July 1922)

I. "From the Dark"

The first of this six-part series deals with Herbert West, a medical student at Miskatonic University who is engaged in a Frankenstein-like attempt to reanimate the dead. Unfortunately for West and his assistant, neither is really prepared for the consequences of the experiment.

Figure 14. Samuel B. Mumford House, Providence, R.I. "The square Georgian house had a monitor roof, classic doorway with fan carving, small-paned windows, and all the other earmarks of early Nineteenth Century workmanship." Photo by Philip A. Shreffler.

The Herbert West series is of particular importance to the overall body of Lovecraft's work because it introduces both the town of Arkham, Massachusetts, and Miskatonic University, both of which play a major role as settings in the Mythos stories.

II. "The Plague-Demon"

Even though a plague of typhoid has come to Arkham, West is determined to continue his experiments in reviving the dead. This time he chooses plague victims as his guinea pigs and actually succeeds in his intention. But the havoc the monster causes is terrible, and the monster's identity is worse still.

III. "Six Shots by Moonlight"

Now graduated from Miskatonic University and with a medical practice in Bolton, Massachusetts, near Arkham, West uses the victim of a fatal fight in his experiments. This tale is Lovecraft's version of the zombie motif in horror fiction.

IV. "The Scream of the Dead"

In his Bolton laboratory West is again ready to revive a dead man, Robert Leavitt of St. Louis, who has appeared in West's custody under mysterious circumstances. Upon the injection of the serum, however, Leavitt does not articulate the secrets of death, as West had hoped, but instead reveals the tragedy of his last moments of life.

V. "The Horror from the Shadows"

In this one West, now a Boston specialist, joins the army so that he may go to Flanders during the Great War. His intent is to work at his re-animation experiments where corpses may easily be found. But now it is incomplete bodies he wishes to work on, and he finds the decapitated remains of his friend Major Eric Clapham-Lee to his liking.

VI. "The Tomb-Legions"

Back in Boston after the war and living in an old house that abuts upon one of Boston's most ancient burying grounds, West, the cold, cynical experimenter with human corpses, discovers in a moment of horror that his experiments have turned against him.

The fictional town of Arkham, Massachusetts, used so often in HPL's stories and introduced in "Herbert West—Reanimator," is modeled principally on Salem, Massachusetts. Usually, Arkham and its own Miskatonic University are mentioned in the same breath, and Lovecraft scholars agree that Miskatonic University is patterned after Providence, Rhode Island's Brown University, which Lovecraft knew and admired so much. Arkham and Miskatonic University (in whose library is housed a copy of the forbidden *Necronomicon*) play the most important role in Lovecraft's Mythos stories of the four major fictional hamlets HPL invented (the other three being Kingsport, Innsmouth, and Dunwich).

In creating Arkham, it was Lovecraft's intention to project the image of the most representative or archetypal New England town, as well as a locale invested with the deepest of New England's horrific tradition. His choice of Salem as his model was not only the obvious one but probably also the best. Salem is remembered as the setting for the infamous witchcraft trials and executions of 1692, the birthplace of Nathaniel Hawthorne (who used the town in his *The House of the Seven Gables*), and as a veritable stronghold of American Puritanism with its often terrifying conviction that Satan was loose upon the earth.

The history, then, of Salem is at least in part the history of Arkham. The town was founded in 1626 by Roger Conant and in 1628 became the outpost of the Massachusetts Bay Colony when Governor John Endicott settled there. With the fear of the devil and his witch minions ever increasing, Salem was in 1692 the site of nineteen executions for the practice of witchcraft, sentence having been pronounced by the Court of Oyer and Terminer under Judge Hathorne (ancestor of Nathaniel Hawthorne, who later added the *w* to the family name). Some current theorists believe that witchcraft actually was being practiced in the vicinity of Salem (and indeed throughout New England), but it is safe to say that the majority of the accused and those hanged were innocent of the charges. And although the trials and executions were held in Salem, the witchcraft hysteria began in Salem Village (now Danvers, Massachusetts), involving suspects from as far away as Amesbury, Massachusetts, and even Wells, Maine.

In the seventeenth and eighteenth centuries Salem became a major seaport in Massachusetts, developing trade with the West Indies and the Mediterranean; after the Revolution, trade emphasis shifted to the Orient, causing Salem merchants to gain great wealth and to rear the stately mansions of Washington Square and on Federal, Chestnut, and Essex streets.

Famous Salem residents, aside from Hawthorne, were Nathaniel Bowditch, author of the standard text for seamen, Captain William Driver, who named the American flag "Old Glory," and inventor Alexander Graham Bell, who did preliminary work on the telephone in Salem.

In Lovecraft's hands, bustling Salem was transformed into the crumbling and ancient Arkham, a place where the connections with witchcraft and sorcery seem to be a prevalent force even in the twentieth century. But as one reads through the Lovecraft canon, elements of the real Salem peek through the fictional Arkham. In his attempts to make Arkham seem the stuff of reality rather than of dream, Lovecraft went so far as to produce a street map of Arkham that shares so many features in common with Salem as to leave no doubt as to its origin.

Prominent first of all are the street names of Salem and Arkham. Most of historic Salem is located south of the North River, just as HPL's map of Arkham is south of the Miskatonic River. Salem's Bridge Street becomes Arkham's River Street. The two towns have a Washington Street and a Saltonstall Street, while Salem's Highland Avenue and Chestnut Street become Arkham's High and Walnut streets. Also, the names of some of HPL's characters appear on Salem street signs: Gedney Street (for Gedney in "At the Mountains of Madness"), Leavitt Street (for Robert Leavitt in "Herbert West—Reanimator"), and so on (see Figures 15 and 16).

On Lovecraft's map of Arkham will be found Hangman's Hill occupying the same position as Gallows Hill on a map of Salem. There is a Ropes Garrison corresponding to Salem's Ropes Mansion, though the latter is a residence, not a fortress; a Witch House on the corner of Arkham's Pickman and Parsonage Streets corresponding to Salem's Witch House on the corner of Essex and North; and both towns share Crowninshield and Derby houses.

Central in Arkham is what Lovecraft labeled only as the Burying Ground, and in Salem at Charter and Liberty streets is the old Charter Street Burial Ground, where Judge John Hathorne, the witch prosecutor, is laid to an uneasy rest.

With the identification of Miskatonic University as Brown Univer-

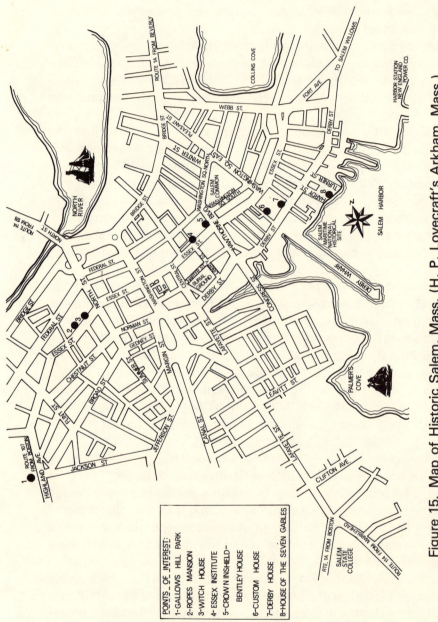

POINTS OF INTEREST:
1- GALLOWS HILL PARK
2- ROPES MANSION
3- WITCH HOUSE
4- ESSEX INSTITUTE
5- CROWNINSHIELD-
    BENTLEY HOUSE
6- CUSTOM HOUSE
7- DERBY HOUSE
8- HOUSE OF THE SEVEN GABLES

Figure 15. Map of Historic Salem, Mass. (H. P. Lovecraft's Arkham, Mass.)

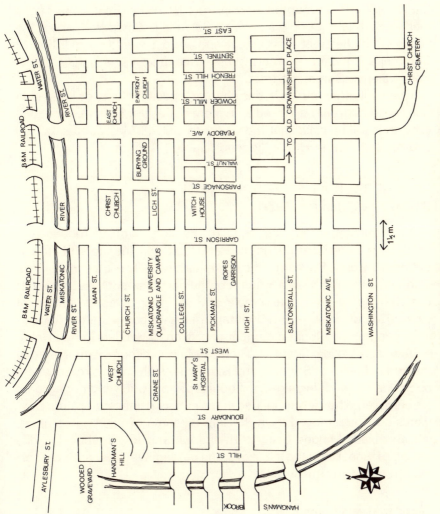

Figure 16. H. P. Lovecraft's Map of Arkham, Mass.

sity in Providence, it becomes perhaps of lesser interest that Salem is the site of Salem State College, which was established in 1852; nevertheless, the latter may have suggested the need for the former.

Of course, the Arkham Sanitarium, which figures in "The Thing on the Doorstep," undoubtedly proceeded from the great irony of the mental hospital that now stands on Salem's Gallows Hill, where the accused witches met their unjust end. And Lovecraft's mention of Summer's Pond in "Herbert West—Reanimator" is surely drawn from Salem's Summer Street.

In several other entries in this chapter, specific points of interest in Salem-Arkham will be looked at in more detail, but from this brief discussion it will be clear that the visitor to Salem, Massachusetts, will find himself also in HPL's "legend haunted Arkham."

"THE HORROR AT RED HOOK" (1925)
(*Weird Tales*, January 1927)

It is against the teeming, squalid tenements and warehouses in Brooklyn's waterfront district of Red Hook that the story of Robert Suydam unfolds. Suydam, who occupies his family seat, a mansion in Flatbush, has long been a student of the occult, and it is as a result of this that he begins to assemble and maintain a congregation of strange Middle Eastern and Oriental ruffians—a congregation that has as its geographical locus a number of broken-down flats in Red Hook.

New York police detective Thomas Malone becomes interested in the odd behavior of Suydam and is drawn deeply into the case when, on Suydam's wedding night, the bodies of both bride and bridegroom are discovered horribly mutilated in their Cunard liner stateroom. Suydam's body is removed from the ship by some of his Asian cronies, and this leads Malone back to Red Hook and to the shocking discovery of what lies in the maze of stone passageways beneath the sordid streets of South Brooklyn.

"THE HOUND" (1922)
(*Weird Tales*, February 1925)

This tale concerns two men, the narrator and one St. John, who have devoted their lives to the study and aesthetic appreciation of the bizarre and the macabre. This pastime finds expression in their robbing graves. During one such excavation, they discover a tomb in which rests a body wearing a jade amulet. They steal the amulet only to discover that possessing it summons forth the one to whom it belonged.

This short story was one of Lovecraft's early publishing successes, and it presents several features of interest. There can be little doubt that it was inspired by Sir Arthur Conan Doyle's *The Hound of the Baskervilles*. Lovecraft admitted to having read and liked the Sherlock Holmes stories, and he even wrote that "I used to write detective stories very often, the works of A. Conan Doyle being my model so far as plot was concerned." Although "The Hound" is obviously not a detective story, the influence of Doyle is apparent.

In the dedication note at the beginning of *The Hound of the Baskervilles*, Doyle alludes to the "account of a west country legend which first suggested the idea of this little tale to my mind." Similarly, in the narrative text of "The Hound" Lovecraft mentions "the tales of the peasantry" that tell of the spectral monster central to the story. Then, remembering the words of Dr. Mortimer in Chapter 2 of Doyle's *Hound* ("Mr. Holmes, they were the footprints of a gigantic hound!'"), Lovecraft includes the following amazing set of paraphrasings: "the faint deeptoned baying of some gigantic hound"; "the faint distant baying of some gigantic hound"; "faint, distant baying over the moor"; "on the moor the faint baying of some gigantic hound"; "a faint, deep, insistent note as of a gigantic hound"; "a deep, sardonic bay as of some gigantic hound." Surely, Lovecraft makes his point.

There are also several other literary allusions that are prominent in "The Hound." As St. John dies, he whispers: "The amulet—that damned thing. . . .'" This is a tip of the Lovecraftian hat to Ambrose Bierce for his story "The Damned Thing," wherein these lines are found: "'What is it? What the devil is it?' I asked. 'That Damned Thing!' he replied. . . .'"

The following paraphrasings and references are from Poe: "On the night of September 24, 19— —, I heard a knock at my chamber door." This, of course, comes from "The Raven." Later Lovecraft writes that "upon an evil tenement had fallen a red death," which is derived from the title of Poe's "The Masque of the Red Death"; and still later, "Finally I reached the rotting oblong box," which *is* the title of Poe's "The Oblong Box."

Serious though "The Hound" may be as a piece of horror fiction, it is hard to believe that Lovecraft was not having a little fun with his readers.

"HYPNOS" (1922)
(*The National Amateur*, May 1923)

The narrator, a philosophically inclined young man, comes across a mysterious bearded individual who is unconscious. After being revived, the mysterious gentleman joins the narrator at the latter's lodgings in Kent, and there the two begin a series of mystical and metaphysical investigations with the aid of narcotic drugs. These experiments take their toll, however, causing the two to age with incredible rapidity. But more distressing than this is what the bearded man seems to have seen in his dreams of time and space, and the intense fear he exhibits of something in the vicinity of the celestial constellation of Corona Borealis. The tale culminates with a dim hint of just what it is that lurks in the winter constellation.

"IMPRISONED WITH THE PHARAOHS" (1924)
(*Weird Tales*, serialized May-July 1924; published as by Harry Houdini)

Ghost-written by Lovecraft for escape artist Harry Houdini, this tale appeared as written by Houdini in the May 1924 issue of *Weird Tales*. The narrative is a combination travelogue and horror story about Houdini's being waylaid by Arab toughs and lowered, bound, into a pit in the desert near the Sphinx. Houdini escapes from his bonds but unfortunately is not able to escape from witnessing an ancient and ghoulish ritual conducted deep beneath the sands of Gizeh.

"IN THE VAULT" (1925)
(*The Tryout*, November 1925)

This is the story of George Birch, an undertaker who is not too careful about the way in which he discharges his professional responsibilities. He has been known, through carelessness, to place the wrong coffin under a particular headstone and to skimp on the construction of coffins. There are also other little shortcuts that Birch takes, but he comes to have sound reason for contrition the night he is trapped in the receiving room of the Peck Valley Cemetery.

"IN THE WALLS OF ERYX" (1935)
(*Weird Tales*, October 1939)

This is basically a straight science fiction story, unusual for Lovecraft, written with Kenneth Sterling. It is the story of Kenton J. Stanfield, an employee of the Venus Crystal Company, an enterprise whose purpose is to retrieve glowing, radioactive crystals from the planet Venus to provide energy for the cities of Earth.

In his search for the crystals, Stanfield comes upon the body of another company employee, a body that holds a crystal clutched in its hand. But Stanfield is baffled by an invisible wall separating him from the body. At last, Stanfield discovers an opening in the wall, and subsequently finds that he has been trapped inside a confusing invisible labyrinth.

"THE LURKING FEAR" (1922)
(*Home Brew*, serialized January-April 1923)

On the top of Tempest Mountain, located deep within the Catskills of New York State, stands the deserted Martense mansion, seemingly the dwelling place of an alleged monster that has brought death to the surrounding villages. It is to the Martense mansion and Tempest Mountain that the narrator of the story comes with his two companions in search of "the lurking fear."

There is a discernible pattern in the monster's appearance. It is always during a booming thunderstorm, and the carnage the monster brings is manifested by earthslides and the bloody murders of townspeople in the area. The secret of the lurking fear, the narrator concludes, has something to do with the history of the degenerate Martense family and with the strange mounds and ridges that surround the house on Tempest Mountain.

"THE MOON-BOG" (1921)
(*Weird Tales*, June 1926)

Having returned from America to his native Ireland, Denys Barry moves into the castle of his ancestors at Kilderry and plans, as the first order of business, to drain the festering bog that stands near the castle. Barry's purpose is twofold; he wishes to make the land under the bog productive, and he also desires to investigate the legend of a city supposedly built by the ancient Greeks on that site.

Lending credence to that legend is a ruin standing on an islet in the center of the bog. It is not until Barry's laborers begin to act strangely and weird lights and sounds begin to issue from the ruin that the legend of the lost city is taken at all seriously. But worse than the flutelike sounds and flickering lights coming from the ruin on the islet is a grotesque thing seen in a shaft of moonlight that falls whitely on the tower of the moon-bog's ruin.

"THE MUSIC OF ERICH ZANN" (1921)
(*The National Amateur*, March 1922)

In the mysterious Rue d'Auseil lives the mute violinist Erich Zann, who can be heard to play the most fantastic of airs. Although he earns his living by performing with a theater orchestra, Zann seems to be an avant-garde composer of the first order.

But Zann's reticence to permit anyone to hear his own eerie music or, especially, to peer out of the gable window in his shabby garret quarters leads to the revelation of a cosmic horror that is only hinted at—but that is only capable of being characterized as having something to do with Plato's "music of the spheres."

"THE NAMELESS CITY" (1921)
(*Transatlantic Circular*, n.d.)

This is considered by numerous critics to be the first of Lovecraft's Mythos stories, since it introduces the mad Arab poet Abdul Alhazred, author of the hideous magical grimoire, the *Necronomicon*.

The story concerns an explorer who discovers a city that was in ruins even in the ancient days of Chaldea. Investigation of the ruins reveals a series of temples with ceilings too low to have been used by ordinary men. In one of the temples a passageway leads deep into the earth through a kind of museum containing the remains of richly dressed reptilian creatures. The passageway ends at a massive brass door glowing with a brilliant luminescence. But what the narrator discovers deep in the subterranean corridor compels him to leave forever secret the location of the nameless city.

"THE OTHER GODS" (1921)
(*The Fantasy Fan*, November 1933)

Beyond Hatheg is the peak of Hatheg-Kla, where the gods of earth once played before man began to invade such summits and drove them off to the mountain of Kadath in the cold waste. But Barzai the Wise of Ulthar knows that periodically the gods return to Hatheg-Kla, and it is there that he determines to discover them at their play. With a priest of Ulthar named Atal, Barzai begins the ascent of Hatheg-Kla, driven on by ambition and vanity.

"THE OUTSIDER" (1921)
(*Weird Tales*, April 1926)

This tale is told in the first person by a young man who has dwelt, for as long as he can recall, in the total isolation of an old castle. The castle is surrounded by a rotting forest so dense that not even the sky is visible. Fearing to escape the castle by means of the impenetrable forest, the narrator determines that he has now come to an age at which he is willing to try to scale the soaring black tower of the ancient stone structure, a tower that seems to lead up beyond the clouds.

He begins his ascent, and upon reaching a chamber at what he presumes to be the tower's summit, he wrenches open a grating and sees the moon for the first time in his life. But instead of finding himself high in the sky, he discovers that he is at ground level on a plateau that stretches away into the distance.

In his exploration of this strange land, he comes upon a castle ablaze with the lights of a great party. But when he enters the castle and confronts the revelers therein, their reaction is one of horror—and the narrator's discovery is a thousandfold worse.

"PICKMAN'S MODEL" (1926)
(*Weird Tales*, October 1927)

This story, rather Hawthornean in its tone and its attention to psychological horror, is that of Richard Upton Pickman, a Boston artist of the gruesome and horrific, who is shunned by all of his friends and acquaintances not only because of the macabre subject matter of his art but also because of the unknown source of his inspiration.

It is significant to note that although the story of Pickman itself does

not make the fact clear, the artist is the owner of a copy of Abdul Alhazred's *Necronomicon* (see Appendix 2).

"THE PICTURE IN THE HOUSE" (c. 1919)
(*The National Amateur*, July 1919)

In the eerie and cloistered hills west of Arkham the narrator is driven
by a fierce thunderstorm to seek shelter in one of the "lovely farm-
houses of backwoods New England." The house, he discovers, contains a singular library that includes a copy of "Pigafetta's account of
the Congo region." An illustration in the book depicting "a butcher's
shop of the cannibal Anziques" causes the narrator a great deal of uneasiness.

Suddenly, the narrator is startled by the appearance of a bearded
old man, dressed in rags, who welcomes him and asks that he translate from the old book, since the old man can plainly see that the narrator is city bred and educated. But the old man's interest in the
"Regnum Congo," and particularly in the terrible picture, is not the
kind of thing that inspires a guest's confidence in his host.

"POETRY AND THE GODS" (c. 1920)
(*The United Amateur*, September 1920; published as by Anna Helen
Crofts and Henry Paget-Lowe)

In this vignette, a collaboration between Lovecraft and Anna Helen
Crofts, a young girl named Marcia has a type of transcendental experience. She is reading an uninspiring free-verse poem, but because she
has such a poetic soul and has brought her own nature to bear on the
poem, she is visited by Hermes, who whisks her off to Parnassus.
Thereupon, she encounters the shades of Dante, Goethe, Shake-
speare, Milton, Keats, and several notable Greek gods.

"POLARIS" (1918)
(*The Philosopher*, December 1920)

As the narrator meditates on the Pole Star, which hangs above a
cemetery and swampland outside his window, he has visions of a
splendid hyperborean city called Olathoe in the country of Lomar. But
an agony of guilt surrounds him because he cannot separate fantasy
well enough from reality to save the city from impending disaster.

Is it the narrator's brick house near the swamp and the cemetary that is real or is it the fabulous city? And why does the narrator seem instinctively to know the language of Lomar? Can it be that there actually is a city of Olathoe that is in mortal peril? The answer seems to lie in the winking Pole Star, which tortures the narrator and allows him sleep only on cloudy nights.

"THE QUEST OF IRANON" (1921)
(*The Galleon*, July-August 1935)

In this tragically beautiful allegory, a balladeer and dreamer named Iranon is found wandering the world in search of his native city of Aira, where songs and dreams are held above all else. In the objectionable city of granite where only toil is important, Iranon meets a boy, called Romnod, who longs to travel the world.

So Iranon and Romnod depart together and arrive in the city of Oonai, a city of song but also of debauchery. Here Romnod perishes, leaving Iranon to continue his quest for the beautiful land of Aira. It is only when Iranon meets a shepherd who knew him in his youth that the pitiful truth about Aira becomes known to the seeker.

"THE RATS IN THE WALLS" (1923)
(*Weird Tales*, March 1924)

The narrator, a scion of the old English de la Poer family, returns to England from Bolton, Massachusetts, to reclaim the ancestral seat at Exham Priory. But he soon comes to learn that the priory as well as any member of the de la Poers is feared inordinately by the locals. The narrator recounts a great deal of family history, unsettling in itself, and proposes that there is probably good reason for fear among the locals but concludes that they are too superstitious.

It is when the narrator's pet cat discovers a seeming army of rats in the walls of the priory that the amazing depth of the castle is plumbed. In an effort to find out where the rats come from and where they go, a number of levels below the crypt come to light—literally architectural layers that recede in time the deeper one goes. It is finally in the vast section of the castle that lies *below* the level of ancient Roman construction that the hideous nature of the de la Poer family is revealed as well as the reason that the rats scampered starving through the walls of the priory.

"THE SHADOW OUT OF TIME" (1934)
(*Astounding Stories*, June 1936)

One moment Nathaniel Wingate Peaslee is conducting a class in economics at Arkham's Miskatonic University and the next he has lapsed into a chronic form of amnesia that does not relinquish its hold on him for a period of five years. Outwardly, the case is baffling: During his illness, Peaslee engages in the most elementary researches into the nature of human culture, almost as if he is studying as an alien might.

But after his amnesia has faded away, Peaslee begins to be plagued with certain memories, memories of dreams he had during his illness. The dreams recall an otherworldly city inhabited by huge conical creatures who tell him that they existed 150 million years before man and have the ability to exchange their minds with other living things both past and future for the purpose of studying cultural history. It is at this point in his dreams that Peaslee realizes that his own mind is lodged in one of the conical bodies of his mental captors and that just such a mind-body exchange through space and time has been made.

Peaslee organizes an expedition to Australia on the advice of two men who have made startling discoveries there, in an effort to lend credence to the reality of his dream-memories or at least to investigate some curious stone structures that seem dimly related to them. But the dream-memories of the former Great Race of earth and the stone structures that support the theory form only a part of the horror involved in Peaslee's tale.

"THE SHADOW OVER INNSMOUTH" (1931)
(*Weird Tales*, January 1942)

The town of Innsmouth on the northern Massachusetts coast is a place that is feared and shunned even by those living in Arkham, itself a village with dark associations. It is in Innsmouth that there presumably survives a sinister cult founded by Captain Obed Marsh, the Esoteric Order of Dagon, that is rumored to concern itself with the sea and in particular with the black Devil's Reef beyond the Innsmouth harbor breakwater.

It is to the town of Innsmouth and into this atmosphere of aged evil that the narrator comes on a sightseeing tour that is taking him from Newburyport down to Arkham. Uneasy as he is about Innsmouth, the narrator is forced to spend the night there when his bus breaks down. But it is not until after he has retired for the night that he learns about the possibility of truth in the legends that surround the town. He also realizes that he is an outsider against whom all forces are massed in this unholy place that always seems to have a hideous stench of fish in the air.

If one attempts to locate Innsmouth on a map of Massachusetts by following the directions given in the story, he will find himself gazing at the tiny village of Little Neck at the mouth of the Ipswich River, just east of Ipswich and north of Cape Ann. Yet, even though the narrator begins his southward journey toward Innsmouth from the town of Newburyport, it was Newburyport itself that Lovecraft used as Innsmouth.

Newburyport, located at the mouth of the Merrimack River (Lovecraft's Manuxet River), is known as the birthplace of the U.S. Coast Guard and is still very much a maritime community. Many of Newburyport's older houses were built by sea captains and exhibit the characteristic widows' walks on their roofs, which Lovecraft also notes in the story. The town is presently undergoing a massive restoration project, but the blocks of boarded-up brick buildings in the waterfront area testify to the accuracy of Lovecraft's statement that "the decay [in Innsmouth] was worst close to the waterfront."

As with Salem and Arkham, Marblehead and Kingsport, the towns of Newburyport and Innsmouth both share a number of street names in common. But more important are the architectural, topographical, and historical similarities.

Out in Innsmouth's harbor, the narrator of the story observes "an ancient stone breakwater," which is probably a reference to the arm of land called Plum Island that reaches north almost completely across Newburyport's harbor. The narrator also sees "the foundations of a bygone lighthouse," which seems to echo the fact that one of Plum Island's two 1783 lighthouses was destroyed by fire on August 8, 1856.

Beyond the breakwater "and far out at sea" the narrator glimpses "a long, black line scarcely rising above the water yet carrying a suggestion of odd latent malignancy. This, I knew, must be Devil Reef." It is, of course, this reef that plays such an important role in the story as the dwelling place of the Deep Ones. As he had done with the Devil's Hop-Yard in "The Dunwich Horror," Lovecraft once again resorted to a combination of locales to yield Devil Reef. It is, in fact, a commingling of two Newburyport points of interest.

The first is Devil's Den, from which the reef seems to have taken its name. According to John J. Currier's 1896 *Old Newbury: Historical and Biographical Sketches*, Devil's Den was originally an old limestone quarry (the industry being quite important in Newburyport at one time). The mining of limestone (suggesting the Marsh Refining Company of HPL's tale) caused a veritable cavern to be formed in the rocks near the town. When the commercial value of the venture waned, the mining operation was halted and a typical body of New England myth arose around the cave to the effect that the devil haunted the area. Today, Devil's Den also boasts of a Devil's Basin and a Devil's Pulpit.

The second source for Lovecraft's "long, black" reef is discussed in another Currier book, *The History of Newburyport, Mass.: 1764-1905* (published in 1906). This concerns what was known as Black Rocks, a configuration of dark rock that broke above the waterline in Newburyport's harbor. It was at Black Rocks that incoming trade vessels were forced to anchor during the epidemics of smallpox that broke out continuously from 1776 through 1788, during which time the town was in virtual quarantine.

Apparently not wishing to leave much of Newburyport's history out of his history of Innsmouth, Lovecraft even made use of the smallpox epidemics, although he relocates them in time to the year 1846. And he also derived the name of Captain Obed Marsh from the actual Marsh family of Newburyport (which had a branch that spelled its name March).

Unlike many of the villainous characters of Lovecraft's other stories, those of "The Shadow over Innsmouth" actually have an organized cult whose name is the Esoteric Order of Dagon. The order had "modified the ritual of the local churches," had come to replace them and, seemingly unable to meet in those hallowed places, chose the next best thing: the Masonic Hall. In the story, the Masonic Hall is described as a "large pillared hall" on a street called New Church Green. The Newburyport Masonic Hall, built in 1928 and indeed a large, pillared building, is located on Green Street about half a block from where Green and Merrimack converge—at which point there are a number of old churches (see Figure 17).

But perhaps the most intriguing and obscure source for "The Shadow over Innsmouth" has to do with the vestments worn by the Order of Dagon's priests, which is essentially the same clothing as the Deep Ones wear. The priest whom the narrator sees upon his arrival at Inns-

Figure 17. Masonic Temple, Newburyport, Mass. " . . . The Esoteric Order of Dagon . . . [took] up head-quarters in the old Masonic Hall on New Church Green." Photo by Philip A. Shreffler.

mouth is clad in long robes and a "tall tiara." Similarly, the narrator discovers among his own ancestral effects two golden armlets, a tiara, and "a kind of pectoral" — all of which belonged to a member of the Deep Ones. This peculiar raiment undoubtedly has its source in a strange and little-known facet of Newburyport history.

Sometime in the mid-nineteenth century a wood-carver named Thomas Wilson wrought a statue of a woman that was presumably to be used as a figurehead for a ship. But instead of going to sea, this lovely statue stood as an advertisement, much like a cigar store Indian, over Wilson's shop at 8 Strong Street. At the end of the century it was purchased by a man named Barron and was moved to the garden of Ellen Todd, where it remained during the period when Lovecraft would have seen it on one of his antiquarian trips.

Originally, the statue had been given a fine paint job, its robes done up in purple and its tiara, armlets and the leaves circling her neck done in gold. In the care of Miss Todd, however, the statue was painted dull gray and brown. It has only been recently that the Newburyport Historical Society restored "The Landlocked Lady" to its former splendor and now displays it in the basement of the Cushing house, 98 High Street (see Figure 18).

"THE SHUNNED HOUSE" (1924)
(*Weird Tales*, October 1937)

Since its construction in 1763, the strange old William Harris house on Benefit Street in Providence, Rhode Island, had been the scene of many unaccounted-for deaths. Numerous generations had suffered what seemed to be a curse upon the house, although the servants had spoken of werewolves, vampires, and darker things.

Even though the entire house is sinister, its most peculiar feature is in the cellar, where odd growths of fungus and nitre form fantastic shapes on the earth of the floor. Sometimes, it is rumored, these shapes are akin to a large, doubled-up human form — and on occasion particularly noxious vapor is reported to hang in the air over them.

Becoming fascinated with these phenomena, the narrator and his uncle, Elihu Whipple, determine to investigate and ultimately to solve the mystery of the shunned house. Genealogical research that reveals much about the former inhabitants of the house precedes a midnight vigil kept by Whipple and the narrator. In the end an ancient horror is manifested, and there is the necessity of emptying six carboys of sulphuric acid into a pit dug in the cellar of the shunned house.

Figure 18. ''The Landlocked Lady'' of Newburyport. After a photograph from the Newburyport, Mass., Historical Society.

The sources and inspiration for this story represent another of Lovecraft's combinations of historical fact and legend. The shunned house of the tale, which may still be seen today in Providence, Rhode Island, is the Stephen Harris house, built in 1764. Thinly disguised as "the William Harris house" in the story, the Stephen Harris house stands at 135 Benefit Street on the eastern or uphill side of the street (see Figure 19). Lovecraft accurately described the house in his story, and it is because College Hill, which Benefit Street traverses, is so steep that most of the dwellings on the eastern side are constructed with their basements at sidewalk level (and going back into the hill), while the upper floors of the houses soar high into the trees. Recently, the Harris house underwent restoration, gaining a new coat of yellow paint, but in the days before this was done it had much more of a dilapidated and "shunned" appearance.

According to a story about the original owners of the Harris house, this building was reared upon the site of an old burying ground from which all the remains save two were removed. Apparently the graves of a French husband and wife were overlooked and still remain beneath the house. Supposedly, when the two children of Mrs. Stephen Harris died, the woman, crazed with grief, was often heard to cry out in French from one of the second-story windows. Lovecraft incorporated this tale into "The Shunned House" virtually without change.

The other element in Lovecraft's now familiar formula of collecting and combining bits and pieces of New England arcana was a legend culled from the pages of Charles M. Skinner's *Myths and Legends of Our Own Land* (published in 1896). The legend concerns a house in Schenectady, New York, on whose cellar floor there appeared a curious white mold that continuously formed itself into the outline of a human being. This phenomenon was said to result from the attempts of a vampire buried beneath the floor to escape. This story, too, came to be central in "The Shunned House" and was introduced into the plot line with only minor modifications.

"THE SILVER KEY" (1926)
(*Weird Tales*, January 1939)

This little piece is half-essay directed against the prosaic world of the unimaginative and half-fiction dealing with Randolph Carter's attempts to escape reality. Carter's escape is effected through his coming across a hieroglyphic silver key that unlocks what the narrator refers to as "twists of time and space, vision and reality. . . ."

Figure 19. Stephen Harris House, Providence, R.I. "It faced south, with one gable buried to the lower windows in the eastward rising hill, and the other exposed to the foundations toward the street." Photo by Philip A. Shreffler.

"THE STATEMENT OF RANDOLPH CARTER" (1919)
(*The Vagrant*, May 1920)

In the custody of the authorities, Randolph Carter relates how he and his friend Harley Warren opened a tomb in an ancient cemetery, a tomb in which Warren expects to find something fantastic beyond belief. Warren does not allow Carter to descend the stone steps into the tomb, but he does keep in constant contact with Carter through the use of a telephone whose wires connect with the surface. Warren never emerges from the tomb, but the voice of something else does.

"THE STRANGE HIGH HOUSE IN THE MIST" (1926)
(*Weird Tales*, October 1931)

This particular story is notable not so much for its plot, of which there is little, but for the poetry of its movement and for the fact that a fair-sized number of Lovecraft's favorite images and themes are brought together within it. Although this is probably not a Mythos story, strictly speaking, much of what it suggests is linked closely with that myth cycle.

Essentially, the plot is simply that a man named Thomas Olney, a philosopher, comes to the old Massachusetts village of Kingsport and discovers an eerie cottage there high on a cliff above the sea. His ascent and subsequent admission to the cottage bring him startling visions, and ultimately he is forced to leave a part of himself at the strange, high house.

"THE STREET" (c. 1920)
(*The Wolverine*, December 1920)

More a prose poem than a story, this minor little piece tells the life story of a street in a small New England town from the time it is the perimeter of a Puritan fortress up to its destruction in an anarchist uprising. Here is a classic example of Lovecraft's mournful pessimism.

"THE TEMPLE" (1920)
(*Weird Tales*, September 1925)

During the Great War, the German U-29 sinks a British ship and picks up the body of one of the victims, a body bearing a curious ivory carving. In the ensuing days, members of the U-29's crew begin to go mad and either commit suicide or are shot by the captain in an effort to restore order. The matter is complicated by the U-29's encountering mechanical difficulties that leave it a drifting, submarine derelict. Eventually, the only two left aboard are the captain and the first officer, who carries the carved ivory icon. When the first officer goes mad and expels himself into the sea, the captain is left alone to await death.

"THE TERRIBLE OLD MAN" (1920)
(*The Tryout*, July 1921)

In the odd and old village of Kingsport, Massachusetts, there lives an ancient man who inhabits a rambling old house that the natives of Kingsport tend to shun. The old man was a seafarer in his day, and now he keeps bottles with lead pendulums in them, bottles that he addresses by name and that seem to respond.

It is the old man and this strange house that three ruffians named Ricci, Czanek and Silva plan to rob. For their part, it is a singularly unwise decision.

Once again, it is the town of Kingsport (Marblehead, Massachusetts) that is the setting for this story about the old man who is "believed to have been a captain of East India clipper ships in his day." The Terrible Old Man is described as dwelling "all alone in a very ancient house on Water Street near the sea," a house that has "gnarled trees in the front yard" and "a strange collection of large stones, oddly grouped and painted so that they resemble the idols in some obscure Eastern temple."

Locating whatever might have been Lovecraft's model for the Terrible Old Man's house in Marblehead, however, presents a problem. There is indeed a Water Street in Marblehead, and it is "near the sea" (and the Boston Yacht Club!). But actually Water Street is nothing more than a dead-end circle at the end of Front Street, which runs along the Marblehead harbor; Water Street itself is only about 150 feet long and has on it only one house, which is not particularly evocative in terms of HPL's story.

However, if we can assume, as we did in our discussion of "The Festival," that Lovecraft applied the name of one street to its own extension, then Front Street becomes transformed into the fictional Water Street. And this theory seems particularly attractive because of one small single-room building about halfway down Front Street.

Nestled sideways into the hillside incongruously among the large Federal houses of the area is the Pirate's Hideout, which is also variously known as the fisherman's shack and the cordwainer's shop (see Figure 20). Several legends surround this tiny hut, which stands just back from what is locally called Oakum Bay. Some say that pirate treasure was exchanged for goods there, while another tale maintains that on certain nights a person standing near the Pirate's Hideout may hear, borne on the east wind, the terrified screams of a woman murdered by pirates and buried in the lower marshes. Indeed, the latter legend was well enough known that Oliver Wendell Holmes wrote:

> Of the screeching woman of Marblehead
> (The fearful story that turns men pale)
> Don't bid me tell it . . .
> My speech would fail.

Although there are only a couple of gnarled trees near the Pirate's Hideout, and no curiously painted stones at all, there is the maritime connection and legends macabre enough to make the place stick in Lovecraft's imagination. Furthermore, we should consider the fact that in the story each of the bottles has a lead pendulum in it that vibrates as if in answer when the Terrible Old Man addresses it. That each of the bottles has a name such as "Jack, Scar-Face, Long Tom, Spanish Joe, Peters and Mate Ellis" suggests enough of piracy to connect the Terrible Old Man with the Pirate's Hideout.

"THE THING ON THE DOORSTEP" (1933)
(*Weird Tales*, January 1937)

This is the uncanny account of Edward Pickman Derby, a student of the occult living in Arkham, Massachusetts. It is Derby's misfortune to meet a young woman named Asenath Waite, "of the Innsmouth Waites," who is at the time studying medieval metaphysics at Miskatonic University. As the result of Derby's fascination with Asenath, their marriage ensues, but it is a union made elsewhere than in heaven. Having come from haunted Innsmouth, and supposedly the daughter of a powerful wizard, Asenath guides her new husband deeper into the study of the occult than he has ever gone, and ultimately further than he ever would have wished to go.

The two main characters of "The Thing on the Doorstep," Edward and Asenath, both appear to have had dual sources. For at least part of his inspiration for the two characters, Lovecraft again relied on the

Figure 20. The Pirate's Hideout, Marblehead, Mass. "... a very ancient house in Water Street near the sea ..." Photo by Philip A. Shreffler.

historical records of Essex County, Massachusetts—and in particular of Salem.

"The Thing on the Doorstep" takes place in Arkham (the fictionalized Salem), and it should therefore be no surprise to discover that the Derby family of Salem had been quite prominent in the town's social and mercantile life as early as the seventeenth century. Also listed as seventeenth-century residents of Salem were Nathaniel and Benjamin Pickman. Clearly, Lovecraft drew on these family names in inventing Edward Pickman Derby (as well as Richard Upton Pickman, the Boston artist of "Pickman's Model").

Asenath Waite, supposedly "of the Innsmouth Waites," probably also had her surname extracted from two sources. Actually, Waite is not an Innsmouth (Newburyport) name but a Salem one. The first time the name surfaced with any significance in Salem history was on June 21, 1774, when a large number of men, including Aaron Wait, signed a document of the First Provincial Congess that called for "a happy union with Great Britain." Later, Wait and many others recanted, and a group of Salem ship captains, Wait among them, took to raiding British vessels during the Revolution.

Then, too, a number of Lovecraft scholars have pointed out that Asenath Waite bears a striking resemblance to Sonia Haft Green, who was, for a short time, Lovecraft's wife. HPL had found Sonia an influence contrary to his own personality, and so it was undoubtedly an autobiographical note when he wrote of Asenath in "The Thing on the Doorstep" that: "It was as if he [Edward Derby] had been really active and properly exercised for the first time in his coddled life, and I judged that Asenath's force must have pushed him into unwonted channels of motion and alertness."

In the late 1920s Lovecraft and Sonia had been living in New York, but Lovecraft, unable to deal with life in the megalopolis, returned alone to Providence. Finally, in 1929, they were divorced. In his story of Edward and Asenath, Lovecraft exaggerated the rigors of life with Sonia. Lovecraft has Edward cry: "She's probably going to stay with one of her horrible groups of devotees. I hope she'll go west and get a divorce—anyhow, I've made her promise to keep away and let me alone. It was horrible, Dan—she was stealing my body. . . ."

However, the fact that both Edward and Asenath are students of the occult seems to lead inexorably toward another possible combination source. It is more than likely that Lovecraft also had in mind the well-known late nineteenth- and early twentieth-century British occultist Arthur Edward Waite, whose *Book of Black Magic and of Pacts* caused a minor sensation in America during Lovecraft's youth (for a fuller discussion of this source, see Appendix 1).

In addition to the actual family names that Lovecraft used in his story, there are also two of Salem's historic houses that find their way into the text. The first of these is "the old Crowninshield place in the country at the end of High Street," which Asenath Waite had purchased and is in the process of restoring. There actually is a surviving Crowninshield house in Salem, specifically the 1727 Crowninshield-Bentley house at 126 Essex Street just across from Washington Square and the Salem Common (see Figure 21). As restored by the Essex Institute, the Crowninshield-Bentley house is a beautiful three-story clapboard building with one of the gambrel roofs that Lovecraft was so fond of. The house is magnificently appointed with a collection of period furniture, and one doubts that Asenath could have done a better job of restoration by hauling in her "vast store of books and apparatus from Innsmouth."

Later in the story, as Edward Derby momentarily breaks free of the domineering power of his wife, he makes plans to move "back into the Derby mansion" which he, too, plans to renovate. There are two Derby houses in Salem today that might qualify as "the Derby mansion." One is a gigantic, brick structure with white columns on Derby Street just west of the Custom House that Nathaniel Hawthorne made famous. This is now, and has been for quite some time, a home for aged women. The other house is the 1761 Elias Haskett Derby house at 168 Derby Street on the west side of the Custom House, and about two blocks from the House of the Seven Gables (see Figure 22). The Elias Haskett Derby house, now fully restored, is an eighteenth-century Georgian home with a gambrel roof and is similar in shape to the Crowninshield-Bentley house, although it is of brick rather than clapboard. Both of the Derby houses overlook Salem harbor and would be fine places indeed to recuperate from the prolonged stress to which Edward Derby had been subjected.

"THROUGH THE GATES OF THE SILVER KEY" (1932)
(*Weird Tales*, July 1934)

This tale, written with E. Hoffman Price, shows perhaps more of Price's influence than Lovecraft's. It is a continuation of "The Silver

Figure 21. Crowninshield-Bentley House, Salem, Mass. "Asenath had bought the old Crowninshield place in the country at the end of High Street. . . ." Photo by Philip A. Shreffler.

Figure 22. Elias Haskett Derby House, Salem, Mass. "We talked as little as possible about strange and unpleasant things, but discussed the renovation of the old Derby house. . . ." Photo by Philip A. Sheffler.

Key," in which the fate of Randolph Carter is explained. Price's effect on the story seems to be the infusion of complex Oriental mystical doctrine into the Mythos of Lovecraft, thereby resolving the two versions of HPL's pantheon of gods (see Chapter 4).

In the story Carter is whisked off through the gates of dream, which he discovers to be the point at which earth's "transdimensional extension" overlaps with three-dimensional space. Carter passes through several incarnations and is transported through interstellar space, thus confronting the universe's deepest mysteries.

"THE TOMB" (1917)
(*The Vagrant*, March 1922)

From early youth, Jervas Dudley has been fascinated by the tomb of the old Hyde family of Boston. The Hydes, noted for their wickedness, had lived in a hilltop mansion that was utterly destroyed some years earlier by lightning and a subsequent fire.

Dudley is drawn to the Hyde crypt and at length gains entry so that he may commune for long periods of time with the dead therein. But why is there an empty coffin in the vault, and with what startling name is it inscribed? Confined to an asylum, Dudley explains the horrible magnetism that compelled him to be in certain places at certain times and that ultimately led to an appalling discovery.

"THE TRANSITION OF JUAN ROMERO" (c. 1920)
(In *Marginalia*, Sauk City, Wis.: Arkham House, 1944)

Set in the gold-mining country of the American West, this tale opens with the narrator's being befriended by a Mexican named Juan Romero. Both Romero and the narrator are laborers in the famed Norton Mine and are on the scene when a new vein is dynamited. However, instead of a rich vein of gold, the blast reveals an inconceivably deep gorge.

That night, Romero hears weird sounds coming from the earth. The narrator likens them to the strange chanting of Orientals whom he had heard when he was in India. Romero becomes obsessed with the sounds and charges headlong toward the gorge with the narrator close behind. Whatever lurks down in the darkness of the cavern is that which is responsible for the "shall I say *transition*—of Juan Romero."

"THE TREE" (1920)
(*The Tryout*, October 1921)

Very much like the work of Nathaniel Hawthorne in its rhetorical flavor, this is the story of two sculptors, Kalos and Musides, in ancient Greece. They are each commissioned to do a sculpture, the best of which will stand in a place of honor in Syracuse. During the project, however, Kalos weakens and dies, having requested that he be buried with a few twigs from a certain remarkable tree that grows in the sacred grove of Pan. The tree that springs from these twigs in Kalos's grave grows with astonishing rapidity and becomes the agent of a bizarre form of revenge.

"THE UNNAMABLE" (1923)
(*The Vagrant*, n.d.)

This story begins with what amounts to a Socratic dialogue about Lovecraft's theory of literature: about new combinations of familiar things, the importance of *effect* in fiction, and the aesthetics of terror (cf. Lovecraft's literary theory discussed in Chapter 1 of this book). In this tale Lovecraft tries to indicate that there are other ways besides formal argument to convince the skeptical of the unnamable's existence.

The argument occurs between Carter, author of artistic horror stories, and Manton, a hard-headed Yankee who sees little point in an author's trying to write a story about a horror that is "unnamable." In fact, Manton denies that anything can exist that science cannot name.

"THE WHISPERER IN DARKNESS" (1930)
(*Weird Tales*, August 1931)

A series of floods in New Hampshire and Vermont causes a resurgence of certain uncanny folk legends in the area, and Albert Wilmarth, a professor of literature at Miskatonic University, takes advantage of the situation to study these folk tales. Wilmarth's interest in the Vermont stories of monsters lurking in the hills and his vehement skepticism concerning such stories bring a communication from Henry Akeley, who lives in a rural area near Townshend, Vermont. Letters from Akeley, as well as a series of photographs and a phonograph record of curious sounds, begin to convince Wilmarth that there is more to the stories coming from Vermont than pure mythology.

Wilmarth becomes deeply involved in Akeley's plight as the latter's communications about creatures from other worlds become more urgent. Finally, Wilmarth determines to visit the Akeley farm to see for himself what elements of truth there may be behind Akeley's mad stories of the fungus things of Yuggoth.

Although the Mythos pantheon god that Lovecraft called Shub-Niggurath is mentioned in other stories, among them "The Thing on the Doorstep," it is in "The Whisperer in Darkness" that Shub-Niggurath is actually prayed to or invoked by the fungus creatures from Yuggoth. Shub-Niggurath is one of the major deities in Lovecraft's Mythos pantheon, and bears the epithet-subtitle of "The Goat with a Thousand Young." Shub-Niggurath is plainly derived from the Greek god Pan and other similar goat-gods that were of primary importance symbolically to many ancient agricultural societies.

In Greek mythology Pan was a creature, half-man and half-goat, that represented sexual energy and fertility. In other countries the stag was associated with these urges, and in general fertility gods and goddesses in the ancient world were depicted as horned. There is a link here between the horned fertility gods and the old practice of setting up a Maypole to encourage the fertility of the crops at the beginning of the planting season. The Maypole was a great phallic symbol around which rural townspeople would dance and sing on May Day as a kind of magical insurance against a poor crop yield. In more recent times, the practice of setting up the Maypole has survived without its original connotations, but formerly, when the Maypole was taken seriously, a pair of horns was often nailed to the top, suggesting the fertile goat-god.

It is amusing to remember Thomas Morton, who set up a Maypole across the bay from the American Puritans' Massachusetts settlement at Plymouth plantation. One can imagine what a horror that Maypole was to the Puritans (who had little interest in fun, games, or fertility cults) when they saw it across the bay, on top of a hill, rising eighty feet into the air and with a pair of stag horns nailed to the top. Eventually, the Puritans, under Captain Myles Standish, broke up Morton's party and sent him back to England in chains. The Maypole, stag horns and all, was pulled down, and Morton's settlement (which had been called Merry Mount) was renamed Mount Dagon by the Puritans (Dagon being the name of the pagan Philistine god of the sea). There is an obvious Lovecraftian connection here in that Lovecraft wrote a story, entitled "Dagon," about such a god and used this motif in his Innsmouth and Cthulhu stories.

By the time Christianity began to replace paganism as a religious force in the ancient world, the goat-god underwent a symbolic metamorphosis. Christians, observing pagan rituals in which a goat figure was being worshiped, assumed that the figure was representative of the devil. In this way the Pan image became the devil image and was thereafter linked with the practice of Satanism, although the goat-god had prefigured Satanic cults by at least a thousand years.

The great twentieth-century magician Aleister Crowley wrote a poem about Pan that he incorporated into his magical practice. Entitled "A Hymn to Pan," this poem is a celebration of sexual energy as this pertains to the forces of ceremonial magic. But "A Hymn to Pan" also has a rather subtle association with Lovecraft. The last few lines read:

I am thy mate, I am thy man,
Goat of thy flock, I am gold, I am god
Flesh to thy bone, flower to thy rod
With hoofs of steel I race on the rocks
Through solstice stubborn to equinox.
And I rave; and I rape and I rip and I rend
Everlasting, world without end
Mannikin, maiden, maenad, man,
In the night of Pan.
Io Pan! Io Pan Pan! Pan! Io Pan!

It is particularly the last line here that concerns us. The exclamation "Io Pan!" is very similar to the cry of "Iä, Shub-Niggurath," which occurs in several of Lovecraft's stories. Crowley's word "Io" may be a simple shout of lusty joy, or it may be a contraction of the magical formula IAO (Isis, Apophis, Osirus—a kind of Egyptian trinity). It is probably a moot point whether or not Lovecraft's "Iä" corresponds to Crowley's "Io," but at least the possibility exists, since Lovecraft may well have been aware of Crowley's mystical Order of the Golden Dawn (see Appendix 1). That Shub-Niggurath is drawn from the image of Pan, however, can hardly be contested.

"THE WHITE SHIP" (1919)
(*The United Amateur*, November 1919)

Basil Elton, a lighthouse keeper who has long meditated on the sea, is carried off one night by the mysterious White Ship that appears out of the fog. On the voyage, a kind of Pilgrim's Progress, they pass by a number of allegorical cities. The City of a Thousand Wonders (the greatest city ever reared) is full of grotesque madmen, while the Land of Pleasures Unattained stinks of the charnel house. Elton lingers for an untold time in Sona-Nyl, the Land of Fancy, where existence is like a pleasant dream. But his curiosity to quest for the Land of Hope to the west causes him to embark again.

The purpose of this chapter is to provide a functional concordance of the named fictional characters and monsters in the stories of H. P. Lovecraft. In addition, many of the historical nonfictional individuals who play a role in Lovecraft's work are indexed here as well. It should be noted that the entries in this chapter dealing with Lovecraft's Mythos pantheon gods are brief. However, each of these entries refers the reader to Chapter 4 of this book, where the Mythos monsters are discussed in detail.

Entries in this chapter are alphabetical. Following a character's name is a short description of who he is and in which story or stories he appears.

3

An encyclopedia of characters and monsters

A., Jonathan: A Salem witch branded by the devil. ("The Case of Charles Dexter Ward")

Abbott: Owner of a distillery near Providence. ("The Case of Charles Dexter Ward")

Adams, Stanley: The name given by the man who picked up some boxes at the Keene, New Hampshire, train depot. ("The Whisperer in Darkness")

Afrasiab: Arab writer whose work is quoted by the narrator during his subterranean adventures. ("The Nameless City")

Akeley, George Goodenough: The son of Henry Wentworth Akeley residing in California. ("The Whisperer in Darkness")

Akeley, Henry Wentworth: The resident of Townshend, Vermont, on whose farm there were the most palpable manifestations of the rumored Round Mountain monsters. ("The Whisperer in Darkness")

Alexander, Cosmo: The Scottish artist who painted the portrait of Joseph Curwin discovered by Charles Dexter Ward. ("The Case of Charles Dexter Ward")

Alhazred, Abdul: The mad Arab poet who was author of the ancient and blasphemous magical grimoire known as the *Necronomicon* (or *Al Azif* in Arabic). Mention of either Alhazred's name or that of his forbidden book is one of the criteria that critics use in determining whether a Lovecraft story belongs to the Mythos cycle or not. However, Alhazred is mentioned specifically by name in "The Nameless City," "The Hound," "The Festival," "Shadow Out of Time." "The Case of Charles Dexter Ward," "Whisperer in Darkness," "Through the Gates of the Silver Key," "Dreams in the Witch-House," "At the Mountains of Madness," "The Call of Cthulhu," "The Thing on the Doorstep."

Allen, Dr.: Pseudonym for the villain in "The Case of Charles Dexter Ward."

Allen, Zadok: The town drunkard and a nonagenarian in the village of Innsmouth who knew more than he was usually willing to tell. ("The Shadow over Innsmouth")

Alos: The sage and valiant citizen of Olathoe in the country of Lomar. ("Po,aris")

Anderson: Head of the cartographic mission on Venus. ("In the Walls of Eryx")

Anderson, Dr.: Scottish astronomer who discovered a new star not far from Algol. ("Beyond the Wall of Sleep")

Angell, Colonel: Commander of a regiment of New Jersey militia in 1780. ("The Shunned House")

Angell, George Gammell: "Professor Emeritus of Semitic Languages at Brown University, Providence, Rhode Island." One of the first investigators of the cult of Cthulhu. ("The Call of Cthulhu")

Angstrom: Crew member of Captain Collins's *Emma.* ("The Call of Cthulhu")

Antoine (De C — —): The young man who learns of the curse placed on his family by Charles le Sorcier and tries to take steps to avert his own death. ("The Alchemist")

Ardois-Bonnot: The French painter whose "blasphemous *Dream Landscape*" hung in the Paris salon of 1926. ("The Call of Cthulhu")

Armington: The lodge-keeper on the grounds of the Peck Valley Cemetery. ("In the Vault")

Armington, Edwin: Son of Armington, the lodge-keeper. ("In the Vault")

Armitage, Henry: The librarian at Miskatonic University (A.M., Miskatonic University; Ph.D., Princeton; Litt.D., Johns Hopkins) who knew enough about the *Necronomicon* to refuse Wilbur Whateley's wish to take it away. ("The Dunwich Horror")

Arruda, Captain Emanuel: Captain of the scow *Fortaleza*, which was bringing supplies to Joseph Curwin. ("The Case of Charles Dexter Ward")

Arthur: Superintendent of the Norton Mine. ("The Transition of Juan Romero")

Asa: The black man who, with his wife Hanna, was the inhabitant of Joseph Curwin's townhouse in Providence when Charles Dexter Ward went to investigate. ("The Case of Charles Dexter Ward")

Ashley, Professor Ferdinand C.: Professor of ancient history at Miskatonic University and a member of Nathaniel Peaslee's Australian expedition. ("The Shadow Out of Time")

Ashtoreth (or Ashtoroth): A pagan god. ("The Shadow over Innsmouth," "The Horror at Red Hook")

Aspinwall, Ernest B.: Cousin of Randolph Carter who lived in Chicago. ("The Silver Key," "Through the Gates of the Silver Key")

Atal: The priest of Ulthar who accompanies Barzai the Wise on his ascent of Hatheg-Kla in search of the gods of earth. ("The Other Gods," "The Dream-Quest of Unknown Kadath")

Athib: The mariner who accompanies Kuranes on a voyage through the land of Ooth-Nargai. ("Celephais")

Athok: A cobbler in the granite city of Teloth. ("The Quest of Iranon")

Atwood, Professor: Professor of physics at Miskatonic University and a member of the Miskatonic University Antarctic Expedition. ("At the Mountains of Madness")

Azathoth: The "blind, idiot god" that rules at the center of all chaos and one of the most important gods in Lovecraft's pantheon. For a fuller discussion see Chapter 4. ("Dream-Quest of Unknown Kadath," "Dreams in the Witch-House," "Haunter of the Dark")

B., Deborah: A Salem witch branded by the devil. ("The Case of Charles Dexter Ward")

Babcock, Resolved: The minister of the Innsmouth Baptist Church who mysteriously disappeared. ("The Shadow over Innsmouth")

Babson, Eunice: A young servant girl who blackmails Edward Derby. ("The Thing on the Doorstep")

Barnabus: A grave robber for Simon Orne. ("The Case of Charles Dexter Ward")

Barnard, Dr.: The physician who stayed with Joe Slater. ("Beyond the Wall of Sleep")

Barnard, Reverend Thomas: The minister to whom letters were sent causing Joseph Curwin's removal from Providence. ("The Case of Charles Dexter Ward")

Barry, Denys: The owner of the ancestral castle at Kilderry, Ireland, who plans to drain a bog near the castle despite ancient warnings of doom to anyone who tries to do so. ("The Moon-Bog")

Barzai the Wise: The self-styled prophet of Ulthar who ascends the mountain Hatheg-Kla in order to discover the true nature of the gods of earth. ("The Other Gods," "The Dream-Quest of Unknown Kadath")

Bennett, George: One of the investigators of the monstrous occurrences on Tempest Mountain. ("The Lurking Fear")

Birch, George: The careless mortician of Peck Valley. ("In the Vault")

Bishop, Mamie: Common-law wife of Earl Sawyer of Dunwich. ("The Dunwich Horror")

Bishop, Seth: Owner of the farm nearest the Whateley place. ("The Dunwich Horror")

Bishop, Silas: The Dunwich farmer who saw two naked figures on Sentinel Hill the night of Hallowe'en. ("The Dunwich Horror")

Bixby, Hanna: Decreased woman whose body was mislaid. ("In the Vault")

Black Man: Either the devil himself or an emissary of the devil supposed to have made pacts with witches. The Black Man is mentioned in "The Dreams in the Witch-House" in connection with Keziah Mason (q.v.). See also "Nyarlathotep."

Blake, Robert Harrison: The writer of horror stories who uncovers what for him is surely the ultimate horror when he makes the grave mistake of exploring the ruins of the old Free-Will Baptist Church on Providence's Federal Hill. ("The Haunter of the Dark")

Blandot: The paralytic concierge who keeps a house in the mysterious Rue d'Auseil. ("The Music of Erich Zann")

Bohm: Crewman on the U-29. ("The Temple")

Bokrug: The water-serpent god. ("The Doom That Came to Sarnath")

Bolcom: An innkeeper in seventeenth-century Wrentham, Massachusetts. ("The Case of Charles Dexter Ward")

Borchgrevingk: An Antarctic explorer who noticed strange scars on the native seals. ("At the Mountains of Madness")

Boudreau: Member of the Miskatonic University Antarctic Expedition. ("At the Mountains of Madness")

Bowen, Professor Enoch: The Egyptologist and occultist who in 1844 bought the old Free-Will Baptist Church in Providence. ("The Haunter of the Dark")

Bowen, Hannah: Servant who died in the Harris house in Providence. ("The Shunned House")

Bowen, Dr. Jabez: The Providence apothecary who sold chemicals to Joseph Curwin after the latter's flight to Providence from Salem in 1692. ("The Case of Charles Dexter Ward")

Boyle, Dr. E. M.: A psychologist in Perth, Australia, whose familiarity with the case of Nathaniel Peaslee leads, in part, to Peaslee's Australian expedition. ("The Shadow Out of Time")

Brewster, Squire: Local landowner who died in 1711. ("The Tomb")

Briden, William: Crew member of Captain Collins's *Emma*. ("The Call of Cthulhu")

Brightholme, Viscount: Nobleman whose daughter married Sir Robert Jermyn. ("Arthur Jermyn")

Brinton, Sir William: An archeologist who accompanied the narrator of "The Rats in the Walls" in the exploration of the lower regions of Exham Priory. ("The Rats in the Walls")

Brown, John: Leader of the group bent on Joseph Curwin's destruction. ("The Case of Charles Dexter Ward")

Brown, Joseph: Brother of John Brown. ("The Case of Charles Dexter Ward")

Brown, Luther: "The hired boy at George Corey's" who encountered the Dunwich monster. ("The Dunwich Horror")

Brown, Moses: Brother of John Brown and a member of the Curwin raid. ("The Case of Charles Dexter Ward")

Brown, Nicholas: Brother of John Brown. ("The Case of Charles Dexter Ward")

Brown, Obadiah: Owner of the shipping company that employed William Harris, Jr. ("The Shunned House")

Brown, Walter: The presumed spy for the monsters at Round Mountain near Townshend, Vermont. ("The Whisperer in Darkness")

Brown Jenkin: The familiar of witch Keziah Mason, Brown Jenkin was a brown-furred, ratlike creature with the tiny hands of a human being, a bearded human face and long, sharp yellow fangs. As revealed in the story in which he appears, Brown Jenkin evidences not only an awareness of self far superior to the so-called lower animals but also exhibits a hideously free will. ("The Dreams in the Witch-House")

Buddai: In Australian aborigine legend "the gigantic old man who lies asleep for ages underground with his head on his arm, and who will someday awake and eat up the world." ("The Shadow Out of Time")

Buo: An "Arch-Ancient" on the planet Yaddith. ("Through the Gates of the Silver Key")

Buopoths: The "quaint, lumbering" and very shy beasts of dreamland. ("The Dream-Quest of Unknown Kadath")

Burroughs, George: Presumed priest of Satan who put the mark of the devil on Joseph Curwin and Simon Orne. ("The Case of Charles Dexter Ward")

C., Count de: See Henri (de C——).

C., Mehitable: A witch upon whom George Burroughs was said to have put the devil's mark. ("The Case of Charles Dexter Ward")

Cahoone: Captain under whom Dutee Harris served during the War of 1812. ("The Shunned House")

Capwell, Judge: The man whose coffin was mislaid in the Peck Valley Cemetery. ("In the Vault")

Carew, Sam: A chemist (druggist) in Providence during the days of Joseph Curwin. ("The Case of Charles Dexter Ward")

Carroll: Graduate student and pilot on the Miskatonic University Antarctic Expedition. ("At the Mountains of Madness")

Carter: The author of aesthetic horror stories who finds a horribly pragmatic way of demonstrating his literary theory. ("The Unnamable")

Carter, Christopher: Granduncle of Randolph Carter. ("The Silver Key," "Through the Gates of the Silver Key")

Carter, Edmund: The ancestor of Randolph Carter who just "escaped hanging in the Salem Witchcraft." ("The Silver Key," "Through the Gates of the Silver Key")

Carter, John: A member of the raid on the Pautexet house of Joseph Curwin. ("The Case of Charles Dexter Ward")

Carter, Martha: Wife of Christopher Carter. ("The Silver Key,"

"Through the Gates of the Silver Key")

Carter, Pickman: A future relative of Randolph Carter in the year 2169. ("Through the Gates of the Silver Key")

Carter, Randolph: Randolph Carter appears in several of Lovecraft's stories. He is the narrator of the terrible business of Harley Warren ("The Statement of Randolph Carter") and is mentioned obliquely in "The Shunned House." Carter is also the central character in the tales of dreamland that are recorded under the titles "The Dream-Quest of Unknown Kadath," "The Silver Key," and "Through the Gates of the Silver Key."

Carter, Sir Randolph: An ancestor of the present Randolph Carter who studied magic in the days of Elizabeth I. ("The Silver Key")

Casey: A factory inspector who came to Innsmouth to look over the Marsh Refining Company and left in far too great a hurry the next morning. ("The Shadow over Innsmouth")

Castro: A member of the cult of Cthulhu who was captured during a police raid on one of the cult's rituals in the Louisiana swamps. ("The Call of Cthulhu")

Chandraputra, Swami: The Indian adept consulted in regard to Randolph Carter's disappearance. ("Through the Gates of the Silver Key")

Chapman-Lee, Major Sir Eric Moreland: A medical officer in Flanders during World War I whose body became the object of Dr. Herbert West's experiments. ("Herbert West—Reanimator, V")

Charles le Sorcier: Son of Michel Mauvais who avenges his father's murder through pronouncing a curse on the murderer and his posterity. ("The Alchemist")

Chase, Dr.: A physician who witnessed firsthand a number of strange deaths in the shunned house. ("The Shunned House")

Checkley, Dr.: Became rector of King's Church in Providence in 1783. ("The Case of Charles Dexter Ward")

Choynski, Paul: A lodger in the Witch-House, Arkham, Massachusetts. ("The Dreams in the Witch-House")

Clark: Keeper of the Frying Pan and Fish in Providence. ("The Case of Charles Dexter Ward")

Clark, Parson: A minister in the hills west of Arkham who translated segments of the *Regnum Congo* for a certain old man and whose disappearance was laid to drowning in a local pond. ("The Picture in the House")

Clave, Sir John: The knight whose horse trod on a "squealing white thing" near Exham Priory. ("The Rats in the Walls")

Collins, Captain: Captain of the *Emma*, whose ill-fated crew does battle with the crew of the *Alert*' and subsequently lands on the island of Cthulhu. ("The Call of Cthulhu")

Corey, Benjiah: Hired man of Christopher Carter. ("The Silver Key," "Through the Gates of the Silver Key")

Corey, George: The farmer whose land was the site of the Dunwich monster's rampage. ("The Dunwich Horror")

Corey, Hannah: Cook in the Christopher Carter house. ("The Silver Key")

Corey, Mrs.: Wife of George Corey. ("The Dunwich Horror")

Corey, Wesley: Member of the party that tracked the Dunwich monster. ("The Dunwich Horror")

Corsi, Bartolomeo: Twelfth-century Florentine monk. ("The Shadow Out of Time")

Crom-Ya: A Cimmerian chieftain of 15,000 B.C. ("The Shadow Out of Time")

Cthulhu: A major god in Lovecraft's Mythos pantheon that appears only in "The Call of Cthulhu," but whose name is invoked in other stories. For a fuller discussion see Chapter 4. ("The Call of Cthulhu," "At the Mountains of Madness," "The Dunwich Horror," "The Shadow over Innsmouth," "Through the Gates of the Silver Key," "The Whisperer in Darkness")

Cunningham, Inspector: The Providence policeman assigned to the case of the grave robbing at the North Burial Ground. ("The Case of Charles Dexter Ward")

Curwin, Eliza: Wife of the wizard Joseph Curwin who in 1772 resumed her maiden name of Tillinghast after the death of her husband. ("The Case of Charles Dexter Ward")

Curwin, Joseph: The magician-ancestor of Charles Dexter Ward who fled prosecution during the Salem witch trials of 1692 and who was engaged in a gigantic magical operation that spanned the centuries. ("The Case of Charles Dexter Ward")

Czanek, Joe: One of the robbers of the house on Water Street in Kingsport, Massachusetts. ("The Terrible Old Man")

Czanek, Mary: A woman who refuses to stay with the little Ladislas Wolejko on the night he is kidnaped. ("The Dreams in the Witch-House")

Dagon: Another Lovecraft monster, living undersea and apparently related to the Deep Ones mentioned in "The Shadow over Innsmouth." ("Dagon")

Danforth: The "brilliant young" graduate assistant who accompanied his professor to the fabled Plateau of Leng. ("At the Mountains of Madness")

Daniels: Member of the Miskatonic University Antarctic Expedition. ("At the Mountains of Madness")

Davenport, Eli: The Vermonter who had written a monograph about the curious folk tales and legends of that state. ("The Whisperer in Darkness")

Davis, Dr.: The old physician of George Birch in Peck Valley. ("In the Vault")

Dee, John: The famous occultist whose translation of the *Necronomicon* was owned by Wilbur Whateley. ("The Dunwich Horror")

Deep Ones: The undersea monsters of "The Shadow over Innsmouth." For a fuller discussion see Chapter 4.

De la Poer, Gilbert: The first Baron Exham, granted the site of Exham Priory by Henry III in 1261. ("The Rats in the Walls")

De la Poer, Godfrey: Second son of the fifth Baron Exham. ("The Rats in the Walls")

De la Poer, Lady Mary: Wife of the Earl of Shrewsfield who was murdered by her husband and his mother, after which the murderers were absolved and blessed by a local priest. ("The Rats in the Walls")

De la Poer, Walter: The eleventh Baron Exham, who fled to Virginia to escape the dark truth of the family seat at Exham Priory. ("The Rats in the Walls")

Delapore, Randolph: Cousin of the narrator in "The Rats in the Walls."

Derby, Edward Pickman: The student of the occult and a native of Arkham, Massachusetts, who married Asenath Waite, a bizarre union to say the least. ("The Thing on the Doorstep")

Derby, Mr.: Father of Edward Pickman Derby. ("The Thing on the Doorstep")

Derby, Nepemiah: The Salem man whose gravestone appears in Dreamland. ("The Dream-Quest of Unknown Kadath")

D'erlette, Comte: Author of *Cultes des Goules* whose name is based on that of the real August Derleth. ("The Haunter of the Dark," "The Shadow Out of Time")

Desrochers: A French Canadian who occupies the room below Walter

Gilman's in the Witch-House of Arkham, Massachusetts. ("The Dreams in the Witch-House")

Dexter, Dr.: The "superstitious" physician who "threw the curious box and angled stone . . . into the deepest channel of Narragansett Bay." ("The Haunter of the Dark")

Dexter, Knight: Keeper of the Bay and Book in Providence during the time of Joseph Curwin. ("The Case of Charles Dexter Ward")

Dexter, Mercy: Sister of Rhoby Harris who took charge of William Harris, Jr., after the death of his mother. ("The Shunned House")

Dexter, Professor: Zoologist at Miskatonic University. ("The Whisperer in Darkness")

Dholes (or Doels): Huge burrowing things on the planet Yaddith. ("The Dream-Quest of Unknown Kadath," "Through the Gates of the Silver Key," "The Whisperer in Darkness")

Dombrowski: Landlord of the Witch-House in Arkham, Massachusetts. ("The Dreams in the Witch-House")

Donovan: Crew member of Captain Collins's *Emma*. ("The Call of Cthulhu")

Dorieb: Monarch of Cathuria. ("The White Ship")

Douglas, Captain: Captain of the brig *Arkham* on the Miskatonic University Antarctic Expedition. ("At the Mountains of Madness")

Douglass: Owner of the Histrionick Academy in Providence. ("The Case of Charles Dexter Ward")

Doyle, Mayor: The mayor of Providence who was consulted by a secret committee in 1876 about the disappearance of six people in the Federal Hill area. ("The Haunter of the Dark")

Drowne, Dr.: Minister of the Fourth Baptist Church in Providence who preached a sermon against the Starry Wisdom sect in 1844. ("The Haunter of the Dark")

Dudley, Jervas: A Boston dreamer, mystic, and visionary, Dudley is the young man obsessed with the colonial tomb of the wicked Hyde family. ("The Tomb")

Durfee: Judge in Providence. Owner of the famous Judge Durfee House. ("The Case of Charles Dexter Ward")

Durfee, Eleazar: "A school teacher of middle age" who died horribly in the Harris house of Providence. ("The Shunned House")

Dwight, Frederick N.: An employee of the Venus Crystal Company whose body is discovered just inside an invisible maze on the planet Venus by Kenton Stanfield. ("In the Walls of Eryx")

Dwight, Walter: The artist who restored the painting of Joseph Curwin. ("The Case of Charles Dexter Ward")

Dyer: Member of the Miskatonic University Antarctic Expedition, possibly Professor William Dyer (q.v.). ("At the Mountains of Madness")

Dyer, Professor William: Professor of geology at Miskatonic University and a member of Nathaniel Peaslee's Australian expedition. ("The Shadow Out of Time")

Eddy, Orrin B.: Presumably either a member of the Starry Wisdom sect or one who knew a great deal about it and in 1857 told about the sect's practices. ("The Haunter of the Dark")

Eliot, Matt: First mate of Captain Obed Marsh whose duties presumably rotated among the brigantine *Columbia*, the brig *Hetty*, and the barque *Sumatra Queen*. ("The Shadow over Innsmouth")

Ellery, Professor: A professor of chemistry, presumably at Miskatonic University in Arkham, Massachusetts. ("The Dreams in the Witch-House")

Elton, Basil: The lighthouse keeper in "The White Ship" who embarks on an allegorical journey that ends in disaster.

Elwood, Frank: A roomer in the Keziah Mason house in Arkham,

Massachusetts. ("The Dreams in the Witch-House")

Farr, Fred: Member of the party that tracked the Dunwich monster. ("The Dunwich Horror")

Feeney, Francis X.: Member of the Starry Wisdom sect who had joined in 1849 and confessed this on his deathbed to Father O'Malley. ("The Haunter of the Dark")

Fenner, Arthur: A Pautuxet farmer who witnessed the explosion at the Curwin house on the night of the raid. ("The Case of Charles Dexter Ward")

Fenner, Luke: Brother of Arthur Fenner and also a witness of the goings on at Joseph Curwin's house the night of the raid. ("The Case of Charles Dexter Ward")

Fenner, Matthew: "Little old Matthew Fenner" whose body came under the none too expert care of mortician George Birch. ("In the Vault")

Fenton, Dr.: A member of the staff at the asylum for the insane in which Joe Slater was confined ("Beyond the Wall of Sleep")

Ferenczy, Baron: The Transylvanian nobleman whose castle Charles Ward visited on his European sojourn. ("The Case of Charles Dexter Ward")

Field, Naphthali: The man near whose grave Joseph Curwin had been buried. ("The Case of Charles Dexter Ward")

Fowler: Member of the Miskatonic University Antarctic Expedition. ("At the Mountains of Madness")

Fowler, Goody: The witch who lived near Arkham during the days of witchcraft in New England. ("The Silver Key," "Through the Gates of the Silver Key")

Freeborn, Professor Tyler M.: Professor of anthropology at Miskatonic University and a member of Nathaniel Peaslee's Australian expedition. ("The Shadow Out of Time")

Frye, Elmer: The farmer whose homestead is the scene of the Dunwich monster's destructive power. ("The Dunwich Horror")

Frye, Selina: Wife of Elmer Frye. ("The Dunwich Horror")

Galvez, Joseph D.: A member of the party that raided a pagan revel in the Louisiana swamps. ("The Call of Cthulhu")

Gardner, Merwin: Youngest son of Nahum Gardner. ("The Colour out of Space")

Gardner, Nabby: Wife of Nahum Gardner. ("The Colour out of Space")

Gardner, Nahum: A farmer in the hills west of Arkham, Massachusetts, on whose land falls a meteor that is invested with terrible and destructive qualities. ("The Colour out of Space")

Gardner, Thaddeus: The second son of Nahum Gardner. ("The Colour out of Space")

Gardner, Zenas: The eldest son of Nahum Gardner. ("The Colour out of Space")

Garrison, Henry: An Innsmouth man who disappeared under strange circumstances. ("The Shadow over Innsmouth")

Gedney: Graduate student who disappears on the Miskatonic University Antarctic Expedition. ("At the Mountains of Madness")

Geoffrey, Justin: Author of the terrible *People of the Monolith*. ("The Thing on the Doorstep")

Gerritsen, Cornelia: "A young woman of excellent position" who married Robert Suydam only to be murdered horribly on her wedding night. ("The Horror at Red Hook")

Ghasts: "Repulsive beings which die in the light, and which live in the vaults of Zin and leap on long hind legs like kangaroos." ("The Dream-Quest of Unknown Kadath")

Ghouls: Flesh-eating creatures with "canine faces and slumping forms." ("The Dream-Quest of Unknown Kadath")

Gifford, Jonathan: An Albany, New York, acquaintance of Jan Martense who rode into the mountains on horseback to discover his friend's fate. ("The Lurking Fear")

Gilman, Hiram: An Innsmouth man who vanished inexplicably. ("The Shadow over Innsmouth")

Gilman, Walter: A student of mathematics, quantum physics, and magical lore at Miskatonic University at Arkham, Massachusetts, who takes a room in the supposedly haunted Witch-House. ("The Dreams in the Witch-House")

Gnophkehs: A cannibal, apelike people defeated in war by the Lomarians. ("Polaris," "The Dream-Quest of Unknown Kadath")

Gnorri: The bearded and finned labyrinth builders of Ulthar. ("The Silver Key," "Through the Gates of the Silver Key")

Godfrey (de C——): Son of Count Henri de C——. ("The Alchemist")

Gomes, Tony: The Portuguese mulatto who served Charles Ward at his Pautuxet bungalow. ("The Case of Charles Dexter Ward")

Graves, Reverend John: The minister who christened Joseph Curwin's daughter Ann. ("The Case of Charles Dexter Ward")

Green: First mate of Captain Collins's *Emma*. ("The Call of Cthulhu")

Green, Daniel: A "long-dead blacksmith" to whom a corpse found near Joseph Curwin's house bore a strange resemblance. ("The Case of Charles Dexter Ward")

Green, James: Keeper of the Sign of the Elephant in Cheapside. ("The Case of Charles Dexter Ward")

Greene, General: Officer under whom William Harris served during the Revolutionary War. ("The Shunned House")

Gregory: Manservant of the Tillinghast household who vanishes into the monstrous parallel world discovered by Crawford Tillinghast. ("From Beyond")

Guerrera: Crew member of Captain Collins's *Emma*. ("The Call of Cthulhu")

Gugs: "Hairy and gigantic" creatures that "once reared stone circles . . . and made strange sacrifices to the Other Gods. . . ." ("The Dream-Quest of Unknown Kadath")

Gunnarsson: Sailor on the brig *Arkham*. ("At the Mountains of Madness")

Halsey, Dr. Allan: Dean of the Medical School of Miskatonic University at Arkham, Massachusetts. ("Herbert West—Reanimator, II")

Harley, Francis of Bellview: A Virginia adventurer who mentioned Walter de la Poer in his diary. ("The Rats in the Walls")

Harris, Abigail: Daughter of William Harris who died of some inexplicable fever within a year of moving into the shunned house. ("The Shunned House")

Harris, Alice: The maiden sister of Archer Harris. ("The Shunned House")

Harris, Archer: Son of Welcome Harris. ("The Shunned House")

Harris, Carrington: The last of the male line in the Harris family of Providence. ("The Shunned House")

Harris, Dutee: Son of William Harris, Jr., and Phebe Hetfield. ("The Shunned House")

Harris, Elkanah: Daughter of William Harris, original builder of the shunned house. ("The Shunned House")

Harris, Peleg: Cousin of William Harris, Jr., whom young William often had to visit during his mother's madness and physical decline. ("The Shunned House")

Harris, Phebe Hetfield: The girl who was married to Captain William Harris, Jr., in 1780 when Harris was a captain in the Rhode Island forces of the American Revolution. ("The Shunned House")

Harris, Rathbone: Son of Peleg Harris who was cousin to William Harris, Jr. ("The Shunned House")

Harris, Rhoby Dexter: Wife of William Harris who was eventually to go mad because of the deaths of her children. ("The Shunned House")

Harris, Ruth: Daughter of William Harris who died in the same month and in the same manner as her sister Abigail. ("The Shunned House")

Harris, Welcome: Son of Dutee Harris. ("The Shunned House")

Harris, William: The merchant and seaman who built the ill-fated old house on Providence's Benefit Street in 1763. ("The Shunned House")

Harris, William, Jr.: Son of William Harris, builder of the shunned house. ("The Shunned House")

Hart, Robert: Nightwatchman at the North Burial Ground in Providence. ("The Case of Charles Dexter Ward")

Hartwell, Dr.: Dr. Henry Armitage's physician. ("The Dunwich Horror")

Hastur: A god-monster contributed to Lovecraft's pantheon by August Derleth. ("The Whisperer in Darkness")

Hatch: Innkeeper in Wrentham, Massachusetts. ("The Case of Charles Dexter Ward")

Hathorne, Judge John: One of three prosecutors at the Salem witch trials, mentioned in both "The Case of Charles Dexter Ward" and "The Dreams in the Witch-House."

Hawkins: Crew member of Captain Collins's *Emma*. ("The Call of Cthulhu")

Heinrich, Karl, Graf von Altberg-Ehrenstein: Captain of the U-29. ("The Temple")

Henri (de C— —): The count upon whose house a curse was pronounced by a sorcerer. ("The Alchemist")

Herrero, Estaban: Son of Mrs. Herrero. ("Cool Air")

Herrero, Mrs: The landlady of the Fourteenth Street residence of Dr. Muñoz in New York City. ("Cool Air")

Hetfield, Phebe: See Harris, Phebe Hetfield.

Hill, Lieutenant Ronald: The World War I flying ace who aids Herbert West by losing control of the aeroplane in which Hill and Major Clapham-Lee are riding. ("Herbert West—Reanimator, V")

Hiram: Servant of Jervas Dudley. ("The Tomb")

Hoadley, Reverend Abijah: The Congregationalist minister who delivered a sermon in 1747 about the menace of demonic forces in Dunwich, Massachusetts. ("The Dunwich Horror")

Holt, Captain Ebenezer: The Salem seaman who traded a rare copy of Pagafetta's *Regnum Congo* to the ragged old man who lives in the backwoods country west of Arkham. ("The Picture in the House")

Hopkins, Dr. Chad: The physician who issued the death certificates for a number of fever victims in Providence in 1804 and noted that four persons had died "unaccountably lacking in blood." ("The Shunned House")

Hopkins, Esah: Brother of Stephen Hopkins and a member of the Curwin raid. ("The Case of Charles Dexter Ward")

Hopkins, Stephen: Ex-governor of the Rhode Island colony and a member of the Curwin raid. ("The Case of Charles Dexter Ward")

Hoppin, Aaron: Great-grandson of Daniel Green and a supercargo in the employ of Joseph Curwin. ("The Case of Charles Dexter Ward")

Houdini, Harry: The ostensible first-person narrator of "Imprisoned with the Pharoahs."

Houghton, Dr.: A physician in Aylesbury summoned by Wilbur Whateley to tend to the dying old Whateley. ("The Dunwich Horror")

Hounds of Tindalos: Monsters, presumably canine, contributed to Lovecraft's Mythos by Frank Belknap Long. ("The Whisperer in Darkness")

How, Amity: Woman who testified against the witches in Judge Hathorne's court at Salem, Massachusetts. ("The Case of Charles Dexter Ward")

Hutchins, Elam: The farmer whose collie was shot by Wilbur Whateley. ("The Dunwich Horror")

Hutchins, Sam: Member of the party that tracked the Dunwich monster. ("The Dunwich Horror")

Hutchins, Will: Member of the party that tracked the Dunwich monster. ("The Dunwich Horror")

Hutchinson, Edward: A Salem, Massachusetts, wizard and associate of Joseph Curwin. ("The Case of Charles Dexter Ward")

Hyde, Geoffrey: Member of the Hyde family who came from Sussex to America, where he died within a few years. ("The Tomb")

Hyde, Jervas: Another of the Hyde family whose soul was restless. ("The Tomb")

Hypnos: The god of sleep. ("Hypnos")

Inutos: The "squat, hellish yellow fiends" that were advancing on the city of Olathoe in the country of Lomar. ("Polaris," "The Shadow Out of Time")

Iranon: The singer and poet who travels in search of his native land of Aira, where life is lived for poetry and dreams. ("The Quest of Iranon")

Ives, Dr. Job: The physician who diagnosed the cause of death in Ruth and Abigail Harris in 1763. ("The Shunned House")

Iwanicki, Father: The priest of St. Stanislaus's Church in Arkham, Massachusetts. ("The Dreams in the Witch-House")

Jackson, Stephen: Master of the school attended by Eliza Tillinghast. ("The Case of Charles Dexter Ward")

Jenckes, Daniel: Bookshop owner in eighteenth-century Providence. ("The Case of Charles Dexter Ward")

Jermyn, Alfred: Father of Arthur Jermyn. ("Arthur Jermyn")

Jermyn, Arthur: The Oxford-educated descendant of a long line of African explorers who, in investigating the causes for his ancestors' madness, discovers a secret too terrible for a living man to bear. ("Arthur Jermyn")

Jermyn, Neville: Son of Sir Robert Jermyn who died as Sir Robert attempted to kill Neville's son. ("Arthur Jermyn")

Jermyn, Philip: Son of Sir Wade Jermyn. ("Arthur Jermyn")

Jermyn, Robert: Son of Philip Jermyn. ("Arthur Jermyn")

Jermyn, Sir Wade: African explorer who supposedly discovered a race of white apes. ("Arthur Jermyn")

Johansen, Gustaf: Second mate, and subsequently commander, of the *Emma* and then the *Alert*. ("The Call of Cthulhu")

Kalos: One of two sculptors in ancient Arcadia commissioned to create a statue of Tyche to stand in Syracuse. ("The Tree")

Keezar, Alice: See Peaslee, Alice Keezar.

Khephnes: An Egyptian of the Fourteenth Dynasty. ("The Shadow Out of Time")

Klarkash-Ton: A high priest of fabled Atlantis who had preserved the "Commorian myth-cycle." ("The Whisperer in Darkness")

Klenze, Lieutenant: First officer of the U-29. ("The Temple")

Koening: Division commander for the Venus Crystal Company. ("In the Walls of Eryx")

Kranon: Burgomaster of Ulthar. ("The Cats of Ulthar")

Kuranes: The dreamer who creates the dream world of Celephais ("Celephais"). The king of Celephais. ("The Dream-Quest of Unknown Kadath")

Lake, Professor: Professor of biology at Miskatonic University and a member of the Miskatonic Antarctic Expedition whose subexpedition perishes to a man. ("At the Mountains of Madness")

Lanigan: Possibly a newspaperman or a policeman in Providence who was asked by Edwin Lillibridge for a photograph of the Free-Will Baptist Church taken in 1851. ("The Haunter of the Dark")

Larsen: Sailor on the brig *Arkham*. ("At the Mountains of Madness")

Lathi: Ruler of Thalarion. ("The Dream-Quest of Unknown Kadath")

Lawson, Hepzibah: Woman who testified in Judge Hathorne's court at Salem. ("The Case of Charles Dexter Ward")

Leavitt, Robert: The former St. Louisan upon whose corpse Dr. Herbert West performs his reanimation experiment. ("Herbert West— Reanimator, IV")

Legrasse, Inspector John Raymond: A New Orleans police inspector who breaks up a weird pagan ritual in the Louisiana swamp, and subsequently seeks out Professor Angell in an effort to explain a strange stone idol that has come into his possession. ("The Call of Cthulhu")

Lemdin, Fred: Nightwatchman at Rhodes. ("The Case of Charles Dexter Ward")

Leshe, Captain Harry: Navy captain who captured the Spanish ship bringing supplies to Joseph Curwin. ("The Case of Charles Dexter Ward")

Lideason, Eli: Servant who died in the Harris house in Providence. ("The Shunned House")

Lillibridge, Edwin M.: A reporter for the *Providence Telegram* who in 1893 attempted to get the full story on the presumed haunting at the Free-Will Baptist Church in Providence. ("The Haunter of the Dark")

Lobon: One of three chief gods of Sarnath. ("The Doom That Came to Sarnath")

Low, Zenas: A new servant obtained by Mercy Dexter. ("The Shunned House")

Lyman, Dr.: An eminent Boston psychiatrist called in to study the madness of Charles Ward. ("The Case of Charles Dexter Ward")

McGregor Boys: Two brothers who, while out hunting woodchuck near the Nahum Gardner farm, come across "a very peculiar specimen" of woodchuck. ("The Colour Out of Space")

Mackenzie, Robert B. F.: The Australian who first discovered the mysterious stone blocks in that continent's desert and linked them with the case of Nathaniel Wingate Peaslee. ("The Shadow Out of Time")

McTighe: The base operator of the Miskatonic University Antarctic Expedition. ("At the Mountains of Madness")

Malkowski, Dr.: The local physician in Arkham, Massachusetts, who treats Walter Gilman. ("The Dreams in the Witch-House")

Malone, Thomas F.: A New York City police detective who becomes involved in the arcane doings of Robert Suydam in the waterfront district of Brooklyn's Red Hook area. ("The Horror at Red Hook")

Manning, Reverend James: President of the College at Providence and a member of the Curwin raid. ("The Case of Charles Dexter Ward")

Manton, Joel: An Arkham, Massachusetts, high school principal who learns in an untoward way of the existence of things he had always been inclined to dismiss as childish fancy. ("The Unnamable")

Marcia: A young lady fortunate enough to be permitted to visit Parnassus and to meet the literary folk thereupon. ("Poetry and the Gods")

Marigny, Etienne-Laurent de: New Orleans mystic at whose house the estate of Randolph Carter was to be executed. ("Through the Gates of the Silver Key")

Marsh, Barnabus: Grandson of Captain Obed Marsh and owner of the Marsh Refining Company. ("The Shadow over Innsmouth")

Marsh, Enoch: The father-in-law of Benjamin Orne and supposedly a resident of New Hampshire. ("The Shadow over Innsmouth")

Marsh, Lydia Meserve: Mother-in-law of Benjamin Orne and supposedly a resident of New Hampshire with her husband Enoch Marsh. ("The Shadow over Innsmouth")

Marsh, Captain Obed: The sea captain and merchantman who established the Esoteric Order of Dagon at Innsmouth, Massachusetts. ("The Shadow over Innsmouth")

Marsh, Onesiphorus: Son of Captain Obed Marsh. ("The Shadow over Innsmouth")

Martense, Gerrit: Builder of the 1670 Martense mansion on Tempest Mountain in the Catskills. ("The Lurking Fear")

Martense, Jan: The scion of the Martense family who left the ancestral home to fight in the Revolution only to be killed upon his return. ("The Lurking Fear")

Martin, Esdras: Captain of Obed Marsh's barkentine *Malay Bride*. ("The Shadow over Innsmouth")

Mason, Keziah: The witch, condemned during the hysteria of 1692, who inhabited what came to be known as the Witch-House in Arkham, Massachusetts. Keziah's secret cult name was Nahab, and she had taken the traditional oath to and had signed the black book of the Black Man of the Sabbath. ("The Dreams in the Witch-House")

Mather, Cotton: Cotton Mather and his brother Increase Mather were both prominent Puritan period clergymen, and both figured as theological experts in the prosecution of the Salem witch suspects. Cotton Mather was the author of several treatises on witchcraft, including *Memorable Providences Relating to Witchcrafts* and *Possessions and Wonders of the Invisible World.* Mather is referred to by R. U. Pickman as having looked on as an ancestor of Pickman's was hanged for witchcraft at Salem and he is mentioned in several other of Lovecraft's New England stories. ("Pickman's Model," "The Case of Charles Dexter Ward," "Dreams in the Witch-House," "The Picture in the House," "The Unnamable")

Mathewson, Captain James: Member of the raiding party on Joseph Curwin's Pautuxet cottage. ("The Case of Charles Dexter Ward")

Matsugawa: Cartographer of Venus. ("In the Walls of Eryx")

Mauvais, Michel: The wizard whose death provokes a curse on the house of the Counts de C——. ("The Alchemist")

Mawson, Sir Douglas: The British explorer whose expedition was working in Queen Mary's Land at the time the Miskatonic University Expedition was in Antarctica. ("At the Mountains of Madness")

Mazurewicz, Joe: A "loom-fixer" who occupies a ground-floor room in Arkham's Witch-House. ("The Dreams in the Witch-House")

Menes: The little boy who brings mysterious forces down on Ulthar when his kitten disappears. ("The Cats of Ulthar")

Merluzzo, Father: The priest of Spirito Santo Church called upon by the people of Federal Hill to exorcise the demon in the old Free-Will Baptist Church in Providence. ("The Haunter of the Dark")

Merritt, John: The scholar who paid a visit to the home of Joseph

Curwin in Providence only to make discoveries that he did not like. ("The Case of Charles Dexter Ward")

Mi-Go: Monsters linked by Lovecraft to the Abominable Snowmen of the Himalayas. ("At the Mountains of Madness," "The Whisperer in Darkness")

Miller, Wesley P.: Superintendent of Group A, Venus Crystal Company. ("In the Walls of Eryx")

Mills: Member of the Miskatonic Expedition. ("At the Mountains of Madness")

Minot, Joe: A friend of Richard Pickman who came to shun the artist. ("Pickman's Model")

Monohan, Patrolman William J.: A police officer of Providence's Central Station who had paused to inspect the crowd that gathered on Federal Hill the night of the renewed bizarre occurrences there. ("The Haunter of the Dark")

Montagny, Pierre-Louis: An aged Frenchman of Louis XIII's time. ("The Shadow out of Time")

Morgan, Dr. Francis: A professor at Miskatonic University who witnessed the unbelievable occurrence in the university library. ("The Dunwich Horror")

Moulton: A pilot on the Miskatonic University Antarctic Expedition. ("At the Mountains of Madness")

Mowry: The Innsmouth selectman who tried to investigate the odd business going on in that town. ("The Shadow over Innsmouth")

Muller: Boatswain of the U-29 ("The Temple")

Muñoz, Dr.: The Spanish physician living in New York City who is afflicted with a malady that requires his living in low temperatures. ("Cool Air")

Munroe, Arthur: A journalist sent to cover the grim business at the

Martense mansion on Tempest Mountain. ("The Lurking Fear")

Musides: A sculptor commissioned, like his friend Kalos of Arcadia, to carve a great statue of Tyche that was to be exhibited in Syracuse. ("The Tree")

Mwanu: An aged chief among the Congolese Kaliris. ("Arthur Jermyn")

Nahab: Secret witch name of Keziah Mason (q.v.). ("Dreams in the Witch-House")

Night-Gaunts: Faceless, flying rubbery things, unpleasantly thin and propelled by huge membranous wings. ("The Dream-Quest of Unknown Kadath")

Nightingale: Keeper of the Frying Pan and Fish in Providence. ("The Case of Charles Dexter Ward")

Nith: Notary in Ulthar. ("The Cats of Ulthar")

Nodens: The great, hoary Lord of the Abyss. For further discussion see Chapter 4. ("The Dream-Quest of Unknown Kadath")

Norrys, Captain Edward: A good friend of Alfred de la Poer and the fellow explorer, with the narrator, of Exham Priory. ("The Rats in the Walls")

Noyes, Mr.: The man who met Albert Wilmarth at the Brattleboro, Vermont, train station for the subsequent trip by automobile to the farm of Henry Akeley. ("The Whisperer in Darkness")

Nug-Soth: "A magician of the dark conquerors of 16,000 *A.D.*" ("The Shadow Out of Time")

Nyarlathotep: A god in Lovecraft's pantheon, described as a messenger from the Other Gods to the world of men. Nyarlathotep is known to have been manifested in the guise of the Black Man of the witches. For a fuller discussion see Chapter 4. ("The Dream-Quest of Unknown Kadath," "The Dreams in the Witch-House," "The Haunter of the Dark," "The Rats in the Walls," "The Shadow Out of Time,"

"The Whisperer in Darkness")

O'Brien: A Bolton, Massachusetts, factory worker whose death blow to an opponent in a boxing match provides an experimental subject for Dr. Herbert West. ("Herbert West—Reanimator, III")

Olney, Epenetus: Tavern keeper in Providence in the days of Joseph Curwin. ("The Case of Charles Dexter Ward")

Olney, Thomas: The philosopher and college teacher who, upon coming to Kingsport, determines to investigate the odd cottage high on a cliff over the sea and learns more of philosophy than is taught in colleges. ("The Strange High House in the Mist")

O'Malley, Father: The priest who in 1877 tried to exorcise the evil spirit lurking in the old Baptist Church in Providence. ("The Haunter of the Dark")

Orne, Benjamin: Father of Eliza Orne of Arkham, Massachusetts. ("The Shadow over Innsmouth")

Orne, Eliza: Grandmother of the narrator of "The Shadow over Innsmouth."

Orne, Granny: The old woman who told strange tales of things flapping out of the mist and into the bizarre Kingsport house. ("The Strange High House in the Mist")

Orne, Jedediah: A Salem, Massachusetts, wizard and friend of Joseph Curwin. Orne also went under the alias of Simon Orne. ("The Case of Charles Dexter Ward")

Orne, Simon: One of the only close friends of Joseph Curwin in Salem and a black magician of note. ("The Case of Charles Dexter Ward")

Orrendorf: Member of the Miskatonic University Antarctic Expedition. ("At the Mountains of Madness")

Osborn, Joe: Member of the party that tracked the Dunwich monster. ("The Dunwich Horror")

Other Gods: Gods of Lovecraft's Mythos pantheon who inhabit the summit of Mount Hatheg-Kla and are responsible to Azathoth. For further discussion see Chapter 4. ("The Other Gods," "The Dream-Quest of Unknown Kadath")

P., Susan: Woman who received the mark of the devil. ("The Case of Charles Dexter Ward")

Pabodie, Professor Frank H.: Professor of engineering of Miskatonic University and a member of the Miskatonic Antarctic Expedition. ("At the Mountains of Madness")

Parker: Crew member of Captain Collins's *Emma*. ("The Call of Cthulhu")

Parks: The man servant in young Randolph Carter's house. ("The Silver Key," "Through the Gates of the Silver Key")

Peabody, E. Lapham: Curator of the Arkham Historical Society. ("The Shadow over Innsmouth")

Peaslee, Alice Keezar: Wife of Professor Nathaniel Wingate Peaslee. ("The Shadow Out of Time")

Peaslee, Hannah: Daughter of Professor Nathaniel Wingate Peaslee. ("The Shadow Out of Time")

Peaslee, Hanna Wingate: Mother of Professor Nathaniel Wingate Peaslee of Miskatonic University. ("The Shadow Out of Time")

Peaslee, Jonathan: Father of Professor Nathaniel Wingate Peaslee. ("The Shadow Out of Time")

Peaslee, Professor Nathaniel Wingate: Professor of political economy at Miskatonic University who suffered a strange form of amnesia for five years, the result of which was a horribly revelatory journey to Australia. ("The Shadow Out of Time")

Peaslee, Robert: Son of Professor Nathaniel Wingate Peaslee. ("The Shadow Out of Time")

Peaslee, Professor Wingate: Professor of psychology at Miskatonic University and son of Nathaniel Wingate Peaslee. ("The Shadow Out of Time")

Peck, Doctor: Physician consulted in the matter of Charles Ward. ("The Case of Charles Dexter Ward")

Peters, Melville F.: The Providence gentleman in whose private collection were the Durfee-Arnold papers, studied by Charles Ward. ("The Case of Charles Dexter Ward")

Petrovitch: Bakery owner in "The Street."

Phillips, Ward: The author of "The Silver Key" and its narrator, actually H. P. Lovecraft himself. ("The Silver Key," "Through the Gates of the Silver Key")

Pickman, Richard Upton: The Boston artist of the weird and the macabre whose paintings were just a bit too real. ("Pickman's Model," "The Dream-Quest of Unknown Kadath")

Pierce, Ami: The neighbor of Nahum Gardner who attempts, to no avail, to save his friend from the evil influences of an oddly colored meteorite that has fallen near the Gardner house. ("The Colour Out of Space")

Pierce, Mehitabel: Servant in the Harris house in Providence. ("The Shunned House")

Pierce, Mrs.: Wife of Ami Pierce. ("The Colour Out of Space")

Pierce, Nick: An Innsmouth man who mysteriously disappeared. ("The Shadow over Innsmouth")

Pierre: Servant of Antoine de C——. ("The Alchemist")

Pigafetta: Author of a tract on the cannibals of the Congo. ("The Picture in the House")

Potter: General store owner at Clark's Corners. ("The Colour Out of Space")

Potter, Welcome: Charles Ward's great-great-grandfather who married Ann Tillinghast. ("The Case of Charles Dexter Ward")

Prinn, Ludwig: Author of the forbidden book *De Vermis Mysteriis*, or *The Mysteries of the Worm*, added to Lovecraft's Mythos by Robert Bloch. ("The Haunter of the Dark," "The Shadow Out of Time")

Pth'thya-l'yi: In Lovecraft's Mythos pantheon she was one of the Deep Ones presided over by Dagon. ("The Shadow over Innsmouth")

Raabe: Engineer on the U-29. ("The Temple")

Raymond: Old man ruined by the vindictive Asaph Sawyer. ("In the Vault")

Regan, Patrick: The man whose disappearance in 1869 near the Free-Will Baptist Church caused a mob of Irishmen to attack the church. ("The Haunter of the Dark")

Reid, Dr.: A doctor of comparative pathology who had "dropped" artist Richard Upton Pickman because of the latter's unwholesome paintings. ("Pickman's Model")

Reis, Abdul: The guide who took the narrator to the pyramids. ("Imprisoned with the Pharaohs")

Ricci, Angelo: One of the robbers of the old house on Water Street in Kingsport, Massachusetts. ("The Terrible Old Man")

Rice, Stephen: In "an awed discussion in Potter's general store at Clark's Corners," it is Rice who reports on the odd vegetation springing up in the vicinity of the Nahum Gardner farm. ("The Colour Out of Space")

Rice, Professor Warren: The professor at Miskatonic University who witnessed the horrible thing in the university library. ("The Dunwich Horror")

Riley, Sergeant: An officer at the Providence Second Station who looked into the attempted grave robbings at the North Burial Ground. ("The Case of Charles Dexter Ward")

Robert (de C——): Son of Count Godfrey de C——. ("The Alchemist")

Robins, Maria: Servant in the Harris house in Providence who replaced Ann White after her discharge from the household. ("The Shunned House")

Robinson: Customs collector at Providence in the days of Joseph Curwin. ("The Case of Charles Dexter Ward")

Robinson, Buck, "The Harlem Smoke": The black man killed in a fight who becomes the subject of one of Dr. Herbert West's experiments. ("Herbert West—Reanimator, III")

Rodriguez: Crew member of Captain Collins's *Emma*. ("The Call of Cthulhu")

Romero, Juan: A Mexican, with a suggestion of the Aztec about him, who falls victim to the lurkers in the bottomless gorge of the Norton Mine. ("The Transition of Juan Romero")

Romnod: A boy in the granite city of Teloth who travels with the poet Iranon in search of the ethereal land of Aira. ("The Quest of Iranon")

Ropes: Member of the Miskatonic University Antarctic Expedition. ("At the Mountains of Madness")

Rosworth: Friend of Richard Pickman who came to shun the artist. ("Pickman's Model")

Roulet, Etienne: A French settler in Providence who occupied, for a time, a part of the land granted to John Throckmorton. It was Roulet who established a family graveyard on the property, a graveyard that was never moved and upon which the ill-fated Harris house was built in 1763. ("The Shunned House")

Roulet, Jacques: French demoniac condemned to death in 1598 but actually confined to a madhouse. ("The Shunned House")

Roulet, Paul: "A surly fellow" of "erratic behavior" who was the son of Etienne Roulet. ("The Shunned House")

Russells, The: Keepers of the Golden Eagle Inn in Providence. ("The Case of Charles Dexter Ward")

S., Bridget: Woman who received the devil's mark in Salem. ("The Case of Charles Dexter Ward")

Sabin, Thomas: Operator of a stagecoach in Providence. ("The Case of Charles Dexter Ward")

St. John: The bizarre aesthete who, along with his friend, steals a jade amulet from a tomb—an act that has untoward results. ("The Hound")

Sargent, Abigail: Wife of Moses Sargent, a servant who blackmailed Edward Derby. ("The Thing on the Doorstep")

Sargent, Joe: A native of Innsmouth, he was the driver of the Newburyport-to-Arkham bus. ("The Shadow over Innsmouth")

Sargent, Moses: Servant at the Crowninshield house in Arkham who blackmailed Edward Derby. ("The Thing on the Doorstep")

Sawyer, Asaph: The vindictive farmer who, in death, was shortchanged by mortician George Birch. ("In the Vault")

Sawyer, Chauncey: Son of Sally Sawyer. ("The Dunwich Horror")

Sawyer, Earl: A farmer in Dunwich and a member of the party that tracked the Dunwich monster. ("The Dunwich Horror")

Sawyer, Sally: Housekeeper at the Seth Bishop farm. ("The Dunwich Horror")

Sayles: Tavern keeper in Providence. ("The Case of Charles Dexter Ward")

Schacabao, Ibn: Apparently an Arab occultist quoted by Alhazred in the *Necronomicon.* ("The Case of Charles Dexter Ward," "The Festival")

Schmidt: Crewman on the U-29. ("The Temple")

Schneider: Engineer on the U-29. ("The Temple")

Scoresby: The arctic whaler who in 1820 made strange drawings of the "dark, unknown mountain peaks" in the Antarctic. ("At the Mountains of Madness")

Seaton, Samuel: Explorer who called at the Jermyn house with notes about the Onga tribe. ("Arthur Jermyn")

Serviss, Professor Garrett P.: The well-known astronomer who made note of the discovery, by Doctor Anderson of Edinburgh, of a new star located in the vicinity of Algol on February 22, 1901. ("Beyond the Wall of Sleep")

S'gg'ha: A "captive mind from the star-headed vegetable carnivores of Antarctica," and apparently one of the Great Old Ones. ("The Shadow Out of Time")

Shaddad: The architect and builder of the city of Irem. ("Through the Gates of the Silver Key")

Shaggoths (or Shoggoths): The ameboid servants of the Great Old Ones. ("The Thing on the Doorstep," "The Shadow over Innsmouth," "At the Mountains of Madness")

Shang: Blacksmith of Ulthar. ("The Cats of Ulthar")

Shantaks: Enormous birds, "larger than elephants," with "heads like a horse's." ("The Dream-Quest of Unknown Kadath")

Sherman: Radio operator on the Miskatonic University Antarctic Expedition. ("At the Mountains of Madness")

Shippen, Doctor: Wrote letters "concerning the presence of an unwholesome person in Philadelphia." ("The Case of Charles Dexter Ward")

Shub-Niggurath: A god in Lovecraft's patheon described as "the Goat with a Thousand Young." For further discussion see Chapter 4.

("The Thing on the Doorstep," "The Whisperer in Darkness," "The Dunwich Horror," "The Dreams in the Witch-House")

Silva, Manuel: One of the robbers of the old house on Water Street in Kingsport, Massachusetts. ("The Terrible Old Man")

Simpson, Goodman: Undertaker suspected of stealing from the body of Squire Brewster. ("The Tomb")

Slader, Peter: The Catskill Mountain man beaten to a pulp by Joe Slater. ("Beyond the Wall of Sleep")

Slater, Joe: The degenerate Catskill Mountain man who was siezed with strange visions of another world populated by luminous creatures, of which race he seemed, at times, to consider himself a member. Slater, the murderer of Peter Slader, was convicted of the crime and sent to an insane asylum. ("Beyond the Wall of Sleep")

Slocum, Charles: Pautuxet resident who had heard of the finding of a charred body about the time of Joseph Curwin's death. ("The Case of Charles Dexter Ward")

Smith, Clark Ashton: Writer and artist friend of Lovecraft mentioned in "At the Mountains of Madness," "The Call of Cthulhu," and "Pickman's Model."

Smith, Eleazar: A friend of Ezra Weeden who kept vigil outside Joseph Curwin's house in Providence. ("The Case of Charles Dexter Ward")

Smith, Preserved: Manservant in the Harris house in Providence. ("The Shunned House")

Soames: Butler of the Jermyn family. ("Arthur Jermyn")

Southwick, Adoniram: An Innsmouth man who mysteriously vanished. ("The Shadow over Innsmouth")

Stafford: "A gentle old lady" who died under mysterious circumstances in the Harris house of Providence. ("The Shunned House")

Stanfield, Kenton J.: The employee of the Venus Crystal Company who becomes lost in an invisible Venusian maze. ("In the Walls of Eryx")

Stowacki, Pete: The man who, because he wants the child out of the way, will not stay with Ladislas Wolejko on the night he is kidnaped. ("The Dreams in the Witch-House")

Suydam, Robert: The Dutch-American mystic and ceremonial magician who maintains a congregation of Oriental ruffians in the Red Hook district of Brooklyn in order to carry out certain dark rituals. ("The Horror at Red Hook")

Tamash: One of the three chief gods of Sarnath. ("The Doom That Came to Sarnath")

Taran-Ish: High priest of Sarnath. ("The Doom That Came to Sarnath")

Tcho-Tcho: Monsters obliquely referred to in "The Whisperer in Darkness."

Theodotides: A "Graeco-Bactrian official of 200 *B.C.*" ("The Shadow Out of Time")

Thorfinnssen: A mate on the brig *Arkham* under Captain Douglas. ("At the Mountains of Madness")

Thornton: A psychic and mystic who was involved in the exploration of the catacombs beneath Exham Priory. ("The Rats in the Walls")

Throckmorton, John: Owner of the original land upon which the Harris house (known as "the shunned house") came to be built in 1763. ("The Shunned House")

Thul: Cutter of stones in Ulthar. ("The Cats of Ulthar")

Thurber: The narrator of the story of Richard Upton Pickman. ("Pickman's Model")

Tillinghast, Ann: Daughter of Joseph Curwin and Eliza Tillinghast Curwin. ("The Case of Charles Dexter Ward")

Tillinghast, Crawford: The scientist who invents machinery enabling him to see into a monstrous parallel dimension that is "the bottom of creation." ("From Beyond")

Tillinghast, Dutie: Shipowner whose daughter Eliza became the wife of Joseph Curwin. ("The Case of Charles Dexter Ward")

Tillinghast, Eliza: See Curwin, Eliza.

Tillinghast, Pardon: Wharf owner in Providence. ("The Shunned House")

Tilton, Anna: The curator of the Newburyport Historical Society. ("The Shadow over Innsmouth")

Tobey, Dr.: The physician who attends young Henry Wilcox during his madness. ("The Call of Cthulhu")

Tobey, William: An investigator of the horror of Tempest Mountain. ("The Lurking Fear")

Torres, Dr.: The physician in Valencia who worked with Dr. Muñoz in his experiments and nursed Muñoz through a terrible physical crisis. ("Cool Air")

Trask, Dr.: The anthropologist who studied the skeletons found beneath Exham Priory. ("The Rats in the Walls")

Traube: Seaman on the U-29. ("The Temple")

Trevor, Lady Margaret: Wife of Godfrey de la Poer, second son of the fifth Baron Exham. ("The Rats in the Walls")

Tsathoggua: Gelatinous monster from Saturn contributed to the Mythos pantheon by Clark Ashton Smith. ("At the Mountains of Madness," "The Shadow Out of Time," "Through the Gates of the Silver Key," "The Whisperer in Darkness")

Tupper: An Australian miner with the Nathaniel Peaslee expedition. ("The Shadow Out of Time")

'UMR AT-TAWIL: Described by the *Necronomicon* as "The Most Ancient One . . . THE PROLONGED OF LIFE," he is the eternal guide through transdimensional space. ("Through the Gates of the Silver Key")

Updike, Mrs.: The housekeeper of Crawford Tillinghast who disappeared into another dimension as the result of Tillinghast's experiments. ("From Beyond")

Upham, Professor: A professor of mathematics at Miskatonic University in Arkham, Massachusetts. ("The Dreams in the Witch-House")

Upton, Daniel: Narrator of the strange story of Edward Pickman Derby and his wife, Asenath Waite Derby. ("The Thing on the Doorstep")

Upton, Edward Derby: Newborn son of Daniel Upton. ("The Thing on the Doorstep")

Verhaeren: A Belgian trading-post agent on the Congo. ("Arthur Jermyn")

Von Junzt: Author of *Unaussprechlichen Kulten*, or *Nameless Cults*, contributed to Lovecraft's Mythos by Robert E. Howard.

Voonith: The howling "amphibious terrors" of "The Dream-Quest of Unknown Kadath."

Waite, Asenath: The attractive young student of medieval metaphysics at Miskatonic University and a descendant of "the Innsmouth Waites" who marries Edward Pickman Derby. ("The Thing on the Doorstep")

Waite, Dr.: A psychiatrist who kept a hospital on Conanicut Island in Providence. ("The Case of Charles Dexter Ward")

Waite, Ephriam: Father of Asenath Waite and reputed to be a powerful wizard in his native town of Innsmouth. ("The Thing on the Door-step")

Waite, Luelly: A young Innsmouth woman who mysteriously disappeared. ("The Shadow over Innsmouth")

Walakea: The old chief of the Kanakys, a South Sea island tribe, who taught Captain Obed Marsh the secrets of the Deep Ones. ("The Shadow over Innsmouth")

Waldron, Dr.: The "inquisitive college doctor" of Miskatonic University, Arkham, Massachusetts. ("The Dreams in the Witch-House")

Wallace, Admiral: Commander of the customs fleet at Providence. ("The Case of Charles Dexter Ward")

Wallace, Dr.: Pastor of the Asbury M. E. Church in Arkham, Massachusetts. ("The Shadow over Innsmouth")

Wamps: Red-footed ghoulish creatures that feast in the graveyards of upper dreamland. ("The Dream-Quest of Unknown Kadath")

Ward, Charles Dexter: The descendant of the Salem, Massachusetts, wizard Joseph Curwin who was bound to discover the nature of his ancestor's magical work. ("The Case of Charles Dexter Ward")

Ward, Theodore Howland: Father of Charles Dexter Ward. ("The Case of Charles Dexter Ward")

Warren, Harley: The explorer of an ancient tomb who is able to relate only in broken sentences over a telephone to the surface what it is he sees. ("The Statement of Randolph Carter," "Through the Gates of the Silver Key")

Watkins: Member of the Miskatonic University Antarctic Expedition. ("At the Mountains of Madness")

Webb, Professor William Channing: A professor of anthropology at Princeton University who studies the stone idol discovered by New Orleans police inspector Legrasse. ("The Call of Cthulhu")

Weeden, Ezra: The spurned suitor of Eliza Tillinghast who determined to expose Joseph Curwin for whatever dark deeds he might be performing. ("The Case of Charles Dexter Ward")

Weeden, Hazard: Descendant of Ezra Weeden who became concerned at the disturbance of his ancestor's grave. ("The Case of Charles Dexter Ward")

West, Dr. Herbert: Medical student at Miskatonic University at Arkham, Massachusetts, and later physician of Boston who is obsessed with the idea of creating life after death as Victor Frankenstein did. ("Herbert West—Reanimator, I-V")

Whateley, Curtis: Son of Zechariah Whateley who sold cattle to Old Whateley. ("The Dunwich Horror")

Whateley, Lavinia: Mother of Wilbur Whateley. Since Lavinia was unmarried, there was much speculation in Dunwich about who Wilbur's father might have been. ("The Dunwich Horror")

Whateley, Mrs.: Wife of Old Whateley and mother of Lavinia. ("The Dunwich Horror")

Whateley, Old: The father of Lavinia Whateley and a man about whom "frightful tales of wizardry had been whispered in his youth." ("The Dunwich Horror")

Whateley, Squire Sawyer: Chairman of the Dunwich draft board during World War I. ("The Dunwich Horror")

Whateley, Wilbur: The goatish son of Lavinia Whateley and an unknown father whose interest in the *Necronomicon* was only a part of the horrible business at Dunwich. ("The Dunwich Horror")

Whateley, Zebulon: A scion of the Whateley family who "hovered about halfway between soundness and decadence." ("The Dunwich Horror")

Whateley, Zechariah: A citizen of Dunwich and a scion of the "undecayed Whateleys." ("The Dunwich Horror")

Wheeler, Henry: Member of the party that tracked the Dunwich monster. ("The Dunwich Horror")

Whipple, Captain Abraham: Member of the raiders against Joseph Curwin. ("The Case of Charles Dexter Ward")

Whipple, Dr. Elihu: A "sane, conservative physician" and the uncle of the narrator who determines to investigate the rumored horrors of the old house on Benefit Street in Providence. ("The Shunned House")

Whipple, Captain James: Member of the raiding party on Joseph Curwin's Pautuxet hideout. ("The Case of Charles Dexter Ward")

White, Ann: Servant in the Harris house in Providence who was the first to start talk about vampires infesting that edifice. ("The Shunned House")

Whitmarsh, Dr.: A physician, and presumably an associate of Dr. Chase, who, with his companion, witnessed the strange behavior and subsequent deaths of several victims of the shunned house. ("The Shunned House")

Wilcox, Henry Anthony: The young sculptor, studying at the Rhode Island School of Design, who visits Professor Angell as a result of certain dreams that he has had and a peculiar statue that he has carved during one of them. ("The Call of Cthulhu")

Willett, Dr. Marinus Bicknell: Family doctor of Charles Dexter Ward who becomes deeply involved in the bizarre doings of his patient. ("The Case of Charles Dexter Ward")

Williamson: Member of the Miskatonic University Antarctic Expedition. ("At the Mountains of Madness")

Williamson, Douglas: Uncle of the narrator of "The Shadow over Innsmouth," Douglas was an early suicide.

Williamson, James: The Ohioan who married Eliza Orne of Arkham, Massachusetts. ("The Shadow over Innsmouth")

Williamson, Lawrence: Son of Walter Williamson. ("The Shadow over Innsmouth")

Williamson, Walter: Uncle of the narrator of "The Shadow over Innsmouth" on the narrator's mother's side.

Wilmarth, Albert N.: A professor of literature at Miskatonic University in Arkham, Massachusetts, who becomes deeply involved in the case of Henry Akeley of Townshend, Vermont. ("The Whisperer in Darkness," "At the Mountains of Madness")

Wilson, Dr.: The Arkham, Massachusetts, physician who attended Nathaniel Wingate Peaslee during his amnesia. ("The Shadow Out of Time")

Winson, Samuel: The clergyman who married Joseph Curwin and Eliza Tillinghast. ("The Case of Charles Dexter Ward")

Wolejko, Anastasia: A laundry worker whose child is kidnaped on the night before May Eve in Arkham, Massachusetts. ("The Dreams in the Witch-House")

Wolejko, Ladislas: The two-year-old child kidnaped the night before the *Walpurgisnacht* revels in Arkham, Massachusetts. ("The Dreams in the Witch-House")

Woodville, James: A suffolk gentleman of Cromwell's day. ("The Shadow Out of Time")

Wormius, Olaus: Famous occultist and translator of the *Necronomicon*. ("The Dunwich Horror," "The Festival")

Yiang-Li: A philosopher from the empire of Tsan-Chan. ("The Whisperer in Darkness")

Yig: A serpent god, the prototype of Quetzalcoatl, contributed to Lovecraft's Mythos by Zelia Bishop Reed. ("The Whisperer in Darkness")

Yog-Sothoth: One of the most powerful gods in Lovecraft's pantheon. For further discussion see Chapter 4. ("The Case of Charles Dexter Ward," "The Haunter of the Dark," "The Dunwich Horror," "The Whisperer in Darkness," "Through the Gates of the Silver Key," "At the Mountains of Madness")

Zann, Erich: The mute, old violinist living in the Rue d'Auseil who makes his living by playing in a "cheap theater orchestra," but whose music is the key to a strange otherworld. ("The Music of Erich Zann")

Zenig of Aphorat: Man who sought to reach Kadath and whose skull is now in a ring on a nameless finger. ("The Dream-Quest of Unknown Kadath")

Zimmer: Crewman on the U-29. ("The Temple")

Ziz, Ali: Leader of a second party to the pyramids. ("Imprisoned with the Pharaohs")

Zkauba: The wicked wizard of the planet Yaddith. ("Through the Gates of the Silver Key")

Zo-Kalar: One of three chief gods of Sarnath. ("The Doom That Came to Sarnath")

Zoogs: The darting, brown forest creatures of "The Dream-Quest of Unknown Kadath."

In *The Bride of Frankenstein*, Universal Pictures's sequel to the original film, the sinister Dr. Praetorius has blackmailed Dr. Frankenstein into continuing those now celebrated experiments with life and death. Frankenstein, angered but helpless to resist his blackmailer, is mocked when Praetorius raises a glass of sherry and toasts his victim. "To a new age of gods and monsters," he cries gleefully.

But Praetorius was a bit late. By the time he was proclaiming his new era of supercreatures, H. P. Lovecraft's pantheon of raving, universe-rending demons was fully ten years old and had already begun to coil and writhe from the pages of *Weird Tales* magazine. HPL's own age of gods and monsters had made its advent, and today, to millions of Lovecraft's readers, the grim mythology of entities such as Yog-Sothoth, Nyarlathotep, and Cthulhu has as much substance as the myths of Greece or Rome.

Then there was another Hollywood maxim about monsters that Lovecraft debunked. This one comes from the original film version of *Dracula*, in which Dr. Van Helsing, Dracula's nemesis, solemnly admonishes that the vampire derives his strength from the fact that no one will believe in him. But Lovecraft's durable demons live on in the popular imagination precisely because we can believe in them, be-

4
The mythos monsters

cause unlike Frankenstein's monster and Dracula, great though they may be in the literature of the fantastic, Lovecraft's creations gibber and froth outside the ordinary laws of time and space and are indestructible. But beyond this there are two other reasons that HPL's monsters seem so real.

First, rather than using each monster once and letting it go at that, Lovecraft caused Yog-Sothoth, Cthulhu, and the rest to recur throughout his fiction, giving the reader the impression that large numbers of people in a variety of circumstances and geographical locations had had contact with them. At the time Lovecraft was writing, this technique of a series of connected weird tales was enjoying a vogue. Arthur Machen had used it to some degree in his British horror stories, and Robert W. Chambers had produced a collection of related tales under the title *The King in Yellow*. And of course there was Edgar Rice Burroughs, who began cranking out Tarzan novels at the time HPL began writing; and various popular magazines, particularly the pulps, depended on a central character. The unusual feature in Lovecraft's interrelated stories, however, was that the recurring figures were not human heroes but fabulous monsters that exist in other dimensions. Instead of having a hero who rises again and again to vanquish evil, Lovecraft inverts this notion by introducing an immutable pantheon of monsters that endures despite the best contrary efforts of many men in greatly varied sets of circumstances. And Lovecraft had a talent for making his fiction look like truth by grounding his fantastic stories of monsters from another dimension in terms of the most common, day-to-day reality: actual geographical locations, recognizable characters, allusions to familiar events, and so on.

Second, and perhaps as important, Lovecraft knew how to play on the basic fear of his readers and to link that fear to the evil doings of his monsters. The method here was to take the conventional ghost, vampire, or witchcraft story and modify it for his own purposes. In effect, Lovecraft says to his reader: Everybody knows that there is no such thing as a ghost, vampire, or witch. After all, this is the twentieth century, and we do not believe in the devil anymore. But what about Hallowe'en, about the belief in witches and ghosts? Why have they gone on for so long if they have absolutely no basis in fact?

The answer that Lovecraft supplies is logical, so logical that we can almost believe it, that we want to believe it. It is this: Although there is no such thing as the devil or a ghost, there are indeed things that go bump in the night. But they are far more horrible than even the devil could be. They are more horrible because they exist! They are vague, shambling things that lurk just out of sight, things worshiped by cults older than man, things that have been on the earth for 50,000 years and more, things that cannot die. Moreover, because these omnipotent beasts occupy another dimension, they become more dangerous and therefore more terrifying than the conventional vampire or spook simply because they are usually beyond the sensory grasp of human beings. One never knows whether the largely undefined Yog-Sothoth, at any given moment, permeates the universe or hovers silently and malevolently just over one's shoulder. And one never knows just when or where one of Lovecraft's demons will reach from its dimension into our own to touch our lives hideously. But one is assured that, occasionally, the undying monsters do cross the dimensional boundaries and break through into this world.

Over the years, the centuries, Lovecraft suggests, the outward occurrences associated with these monsters and their ritual worship by men have been observed and misinterpreted. Christians saw "witches" idolizing Yog-Sothoth and assumed it to be a case of devil worship. Or some dark, amorphous beast might have been reported to inhabit an abandoned church and the observers would say that the place was "haunted," never realizing that they had had a brush with an entity whose dominion is the entire universe. But in order to understand the kind of universal evil with which we are dealing, we must first become acquainted with this world of terror and confront, at as close a range as we can, these demons that drive men mad.

THE HIERARCHY OF MONSTERS

The basic problem of understanding just *what* Lovecraft's so-called gods actually are lies in a complexity inherent in the stories themselves. This is simply that Lovecraft did not plan his Mythos stories to be a coherent and unified literary whole, nor did he apparently map out or chart a genealogy or hierarchy for his supernatural pantheon. Rather, he began working on the Mythos stories by using an *assumption* common to all of them, but manifesting itself differently in different tales. For this reason we shall come across terms like the "Great Ones," the "Old Ones," the "Elder Gods" and the "Other Gods," and we may very well assume that the same entities are being referred to, or at the worst we shall be uncertain just whom or what *is* being referred to. Indeed, most often the term "Old Ones" is used to denote all of Lovecraft's most potent deities; sometimes HPL himself used it this way and sometimes he did not. Then again, the particular deities or monsters such as Yog-Sothoth, Cthulhu, Nyarlathotep, Azathoth, Shub-Niggurath, and Dagon will appear, and one may be completely unable to understand what relationship each god bears to another, or whether they are really gods at all.

Aside from Lovecraft's not having planned the structure of the Mythos pantheon before he launched into writing the stories, there is another difficulty. This one lies in the fact that in some of the stories these entities are described as purely supernatural creatures, while in others they are defined as perfectly concrete, perfectly physical beings from other planets. This basic difference will depend on whether Lovecraft chose to use the creatures in the framework of a pure fantasy story (where magic and so on are real forces) or in the context of science fiction (which in this case involves interstellar space travel and objective matter or energy that obeys the laws of multidimensional space). In some stories, therefore, Cthulhu, for example, is referred to as a kind of god in the sunken world of R'lyeh and in other stories as an extraterrestrial. And sometimes a particular monster will be referred to in both ways at once. The point is that there is virtually no way of arranging a hierarchy or chain of command for these creatures that will satisfy the conditions of both the fantasy and the science fiction stories.

But the Lovecraft reader should not feel completely foiled yet. The fact remains that Lovecraft seemingly did envision these deities as being of the same order of existence no matter how he used them in a given story. Therefore, the reader should be able to study what is said about each deity most often and determine from the texts of the stories themselves how the hierarchical relationships work. In doing this, we can begin with the most powerful of the gods (the ones that seem to exist primarily in interstellar space or a transdimensional extension of earth) and move in descending order down the scale toward those beings that appear in the greatest numbers on earth as we know it (see Figure 23).

When Lovecraft was establishing the basic premise of the Mythos stories, he apparently had in mind two different varieties of the most powerful gods. One group of these was to be omnipotent and beneficent (or at least benign), and the other was to be evil or destructive. For some reason, however, the benign deities were never really developed into a named pantheon. The only one of these gods to whom

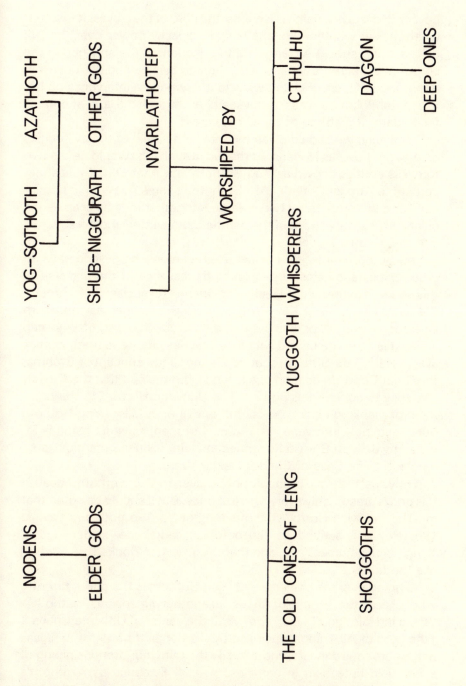

Figure 23. Hierarchy of H. P. Lovecraft's Mythos Entities.

Lovecraft did give a name is Nodens, the Lord of the Abyss. It is somewhat unclear whether Nodens has any special power over the evil deities, but it should be remarked that Nodens is the only god in the corpus of Lovecraft's work to help a human being—and this occurs in "The Dream-Quest of Unknown Kadath" when he intervenes on behalf of Randolph Carter as Carter searches through the land of dreams for Kadath, the abode of the Great Ones.

Seemingly, we should place the most influential of the evil deities on the same level as Nodens. At the top of such a list would be the two formless entities known as Yog-Sothoth and Azathoth. At least according to August Derleth, Yog-Sothoth "shares Azathoth's dominion," and therefore these two creatures together may be seen as the chief administrative gods of the pantheon that enters most frequently into the Mythos stories.

Yog-Sothoth himself (or rather itself) can only be described as an order of existence closely paralleling the essence of the universe as this notion is expressed in Hindu and Oriental mysticism. In "Through the Gates of the Silver Key" Yog-Sothoth is described as "an All-in-One and One-in-All of limitless being and self—the last, utter sweep which has no confines and which outreaches fancy and mathematics alike." Here, Yog-Sothoth sounds like the Hindu concept of Brahma, the Great Good Unification of existence, but the fact that the Whateleys seek to conjure this god in "The Dunwich Horror" to the detriment of mankind places the stigma of evil on it. Also, Yog-Sothoth does seemingly intervene in the affairs of men, since its name is invoked by Joseph Curwin in connection with his necromantic experiments in "The Case of Charles Dexter Ward."

A physical form can probably not be given to Yog-Sothoth, because this god is presumably everywhere at once. But it should be noted that in "The Dunwich Horror" the offspring of Yog-Sothoth and Lavinia Whateley is described as "an octopus, centepede, spider kind o' thing" with a human face, and that this monster "looked . . . [rather] like the father. . . ."

Reigning over the universe with Yog-Sothoth is the god Azathoth, who rules on the "throne of Chaos" in another dimension. Azathoth is "the blind idiot god" who "sprawls at the center of Ultimate Chaos," "the Lord of All Things, encircled by his flopping horde of mindless and amorphous dancers, and lulled by the thin, monotonous piping of a demonic flute held in nameless paws." Evidence of Azathoth's equality with Yog-Sothoth in the pantheon hierarchy exists in Yog-

Sothoth's being the "One-in-All" and Azathoth's being the "Lord of All Things." Yet, whereas Yog-Sothoth seems to embrace the expanse of infinity, Azathoth can be understood to represent the principle opposite this in that he rules at the center of Chaos. This would seem to be a kind of central point in the universe permeated by the influence of Yog-Sothoth. This sort of contradiction is common in mystical tradition, and what the joint rulership of Yog-Sothoth and Azathoth finally represents is a version of the Zen *koan* (a deliberate contradiction meant to be meditated upon, for example: What is the sound of one hand clapping?). The *koan* of Yog-Sothoth and Azathoth would be stated as the reconciliation of an infinite expansion and an infinite contraction.

Directly beneath the shared dominion of Yog-Sothoth and Azathoth comes Shub-Niggurath, called "The Goat with a Thousand Young." Shub-Niggurath is obviously a fertility god associated with the horned deity of the pagan agricultural societies of the ancient world and in particular with the prolific goat, which came not only to symbolize the horned god but was the symbol for sexual energy and the prototype for the Christian devil. In the Mythos pantheon, Shub-Niggurath is mentioned frequently and is never referred to as anything but a supernatural being worshiped in some cases by humans and in others by extraterrestrials. For this reason, he (or she) must be placed high in the pantheon and, presumably, just subordinate to the two ruling entities. Possibly, it is Shub-Niggurath who is responsible for, or who aids in, the proliferation on earth of the monstrosities (like Wilbur Whateley) that are half-monster and half-human.

Responsible directly to the "idiot god" Azathoth is a group of things referred to as the "Other Gods." These are "the mindless and amorphous dancers" who attend Azathoth and provide his chief entertainment through their hideous gyrations and "monotonous" flute playing. The Other Gods seem to play little or no active role in the pantheon or in Lovecraft's fiction, except to say that in the story bearing their name we discover that they reside on a mountain called Hatheg-Kla and that it is death to confront them.

Proceeding down from the Other Gods, and still within the control of only Azathoth, is "the crawling Chaos" Nyarlathotep. Nyarlathotep, with his obviously Egyptian name, is referred to at one point as "the soul and messenger" of the Other Gods, and elsewhere as the messenger between the world of human beings and the world of the gods. Nyarlathotep is known on at least two occasions to have manifested himself in human form, as a man robed in black with jet black yet Caucasian features. This, however, turns out to be a disguise to prevent the humans with whom Nyarlathotep deals from perceiving him in his true, abhorrent form. Presumably, it was Nyarlathotep who came to earth from the outer dimensions to make pacts with the witches of both Europe and America, since many confessed witches testified to having signed their names in the book of the Black Man, who was either the devil himself or the devil's emissary (see Figure 24).

The Black Man was, during the days of witchcraft, supposed to be one of Satan's most common incarnations. It was the Black Man who frequently appeared to the witches, extracting from them oaths of loyalty and causing them to sign their names in blood on the pages of his Black Book. The Black Man was even pictured in certain seventeenth-century tracts on witchcraft, so certain were people of his appearance. He was depicted as a creature with ebony skin, dressed in the long black robes of a cleric and wearing the same conical hat that came to be associated with witches. Little, of course, did those poor "witches" realize that they were not dealing with an entity as pedestrian as Satan but with the ultimate forces of the universe, since Nyarlathotep was finally responsible through the Other Gods to Azathoth himself.

The beings discussed so far are the ones that, in most of the stories, are considered gods in the sense that they are worshiped by great numbers of other creatures. The next group of beings, then, comprise those who worship them. And here, we move from the realm of the fantastic into what some may call the realm of science fiction, because these creatures are all extraterrestrial aliens that came to earth in prehistoric times, established cities, and set up religions from which all of man's modern religions and myth systems proceed.

The first of these groups of aliens is the Old Ones, who "filtered down from the stars" fifty million years ago and built a magnificent black stone city on the Plateau of Leng, which is located in Antarctica. The Old Ones are pictured as barrel-shaped things whose bodies are covered with tentacles and cilia and have starfish-shaped heads. The Old Ones were the first of the extraterrestrials to come to earth, but they were not the last. In "At the Mountains of Madness" the story is told of how other races came from the stars and engaged in wars with the Old Ones until these various factions resolved themselves into a kind of uneasy peace.

The greatest of these interstellar invaders was the race represented

Figure 24. A Witch and Her Master, the Black Man. After a seven-teenth-century woodcut.

by Cthulhu. Under the terms of an agreement made between the Old Ones and the Cthuloids, the former group would rule at the South Pole while the latter would rule the seas. The Cthuloids built a splendid city called R'lyeh, but unfortunately a seismic upheaval caused R'lyeh to sink into the ocean (obviously giving rise to the Atlantis myths), and under this new condition the undying Cthuloids could only lie dormant in their great city, waiting for the day when it would rise again so that they could inherit the earth. Cthulhu himself, referred to as a priest of higher gods (indicating that he was not of the same order of existence as Yog-Sothoth and Azathoth), is even now laid to rest in a tomb on R'lyeh's highest mountaintop, under the surface of the South Pacific Ocean. When Cthulhu is revealed briefly in "The Call of Cthulhu," he appears as an upright manlike thing with the legs of a saurian, a head like a cuttlefish, and the huge wings of a dragon.

Since Cthulhu is the priest of the gods, it is reasonable to assume that the creature called Dagon (who appears in the story of that name and is the object of worship of the Esoteric Order of Dagon in "The Shadow over Innsmouth") is a subordinate of Cthulhu. Dagon is simply described as a man-fish, and his influence seems to reach completely around the undersea world (a large dominion when one remembers that two-thirds of the earth's surface is ocean). Again, it is possible but not certain that Dagon (and the others like him, who are known as the Deep Ones) are degenerate forms of the Cthuloids and are able to exist outside the confines of R'lyeh, even going so far as to come onto the land to mate with human beings. Of the Deep Ones whom Dagon rules, one is named—a female called Pth'thya-l'yi (which, when compared to the word R'lyeh, seems to be in the language of the Cthuloids).

Of the third group of extraterrestrials we know the point of origin. The beings central in "The Whisperer in Darkness" came to earth from the planet Yuggoth (the planet Pluto at the rim of our solar system). These creatures, described as pinkish crablike things, again with starfish heads, are linked by Lovecraft to the Mi-Go, or Abominable Snowmen of the Himalayas. It is unclear whether these starfish-headed things are related to the Old Ones of Antarctica, but it seems likely, given the similarity of head shape yet the difference of body shape, that each group evolved on a different planet, under conditions akin to one another but with subtle differences.

A final major group of beings that, unlike the others, seems to have been indigenous to earth 150,000 years ago is that which dominates the story "The Shadow Out of Time." Members of this group are referred to as the "Great Race" and seem to have had their headquarters on the continent of Australia in the dim prehuman past. According to the story, it was the pastime of the Great Race to collect a vast stockpile of information on the various cultures that exist in the universe. This was effected by the Great Race's ability to exchange minds with any living thing, anywhere in the cosmos. This mind transfer, furthermore, was capable of being carried out across the barrier not only of space but of time as well. So it was possible that one of these beings could send its mind ahead into the future to occupy the body of a human being, while the human's mind suddenly found itself confined in an alien body thousands of years in the past.

It was not really one of Lovecraft's strong points as a writer to describe his monsters' physical appearance. Those entities that seem to be the most powerful in terms of horror are those, like Yog-Sothoth and Azathoth, that are never actually pictured. The descriptions of Cthulhu or the fungus things from Yuggoth tend to be disappointing. But Lovecraft really outdid himself when he drew a verbal image of the Great Race:

immense rugose cones ten feet high, with a head and other organs attached to foot-thick distensible limbs spreading out from their apexes. They spoke by the clicking or scraping of huge paws or claws attached to the end of two of their four limbs, and walked by the expansion and contraction of a viscous layer attached to their vast, ten-foot bases.

This roster of gods and extraterrestrials completes the major Mythos pantheon as Lovecraft seems originally to have envisioned it. And one cannot help but observe how very far ahead of his time the Mythos pantheon placed Lovecraft. It has only been in the past few years that popular theorists like Erich von Däniken have advanced the view that the earth was indeed visited by extraterrestrial astronauts in ancient times and that human beings, incapable of understanding the ancient astronauts' superior technology, mistook these creatures for gods and molded their religions around those mysterious apparitions. This, of course, is the basic theme of Lovecraft's science fiction tales, although it is safe to say that Lovecraft himself, an adamant scientific materialist, would not have seriously subscribed to such a theory. Nevertheless, he found it a sound basis for fiction, popularized it, and beat von Däniken to the theoretical punch by forty years. Furthermore, the concept of spatial dimensions other than our own was comparatively new at the time Lovecraft utilized it, and it is to his credit as an imaginative intellect that he was able to grasp an innovative scientific idea and link it so successfully with the time-honored horrific motif of ancient evil.

LOVECRAFT AND THE OCCULT TRADITION

Actually, Lovecraft seems to have used a method diametrically opposite of von Däniken's in his invention of a demonic pantheon. Von Däniken began with a hypothesis that the earth had been visited by ancient space travelers and then set about collecting data to support the hypothesis. Lovecraft, on the other hand, started with a set of facts—basically that demons of some kind have virtually always been worshiped, often by organized cults—and then constructed a pantheon of gods and monsters that was assumed to be the basis for the widespread belief in certain archetypal deities or that would form an explanation for various kinds of prevalent occult practices.

In both his fiction and his essays, Lovecraft proved that he had a thoroughgoing familiarity with many facets of the occult, but it would not be accurate to say that he was an expert in any particular area. HPL himself admitted that his knowledge of medieval occultism was spotty and incomplete. What knowledge he did have came from occasional excursions into the literature of witchcraft and ceremonial magic, which usually amounted to random samplings of a remarkably complex area of study. Therefore, Lovecraft's understanding of the occult was probably based on data that would be available in any good library and would have included the perusal of the standard works on witchcraft and demonology such as Margaret Murray's *The Witch-Cult in Western Europe*, Sir James George Frazer's *The Golden Bough*, Arthur Edward Waite's *The Book of Black Magic and of Pacts*, as well as, probably, whatever material published by the Golden Dawn (a turn-of-the-century magical society) that he could lay his hands on.

Aside from what he pulled from his own imagination, Lovecraft drew upon at least three major areas of occultism for his construction of a pantheon of deities and the attendant ritual worship of those deities: (1) what is now called the Old Religion by practicing witches; (2) the witchcraft hysteria of the sixteenth through the eighteenth centuries, a sort of massive cultural dragnet that hauled in many more innocents than actual witches; and (3) demonology, the theological study of demonic hierarchies as they were related to anti-Christian witchcraft and sorcery.

The first of these, the Old Religion, is pronounced by its contemporary followers to be the oldest religion known to man. It is the religion of modern witches, many of whom refer to themselves as "Wicca" (said to be a Celtic word meaning "wise one"). The theological system of the twentieth-century Wicca or witches may in fact very well represent one of man's oldest religions, if not actually *the* oldest. "Wiccacraeft" is a variety of the religious practice common among ancient agricultural societies in that its primary concern is fertility, both of human beings and of the crops. To the ancients, whose lives were essentially primitive and depended upon the success of agriculture, the most important principle in the cosmic scheme was the female principle, since it was the female who was most closely associated with the process of birth and generation.

It was for this reason that the universe was seen as a simple duality of male and female power, the sun being a male entity and the moon a female one; light as male, darkness as female, gold the male metal, silver the female. Gods and rituals evolved over the years as a means of celebrating these two principles, but the female was always the more significant of the two. Therefore, for the votaries of the Old Religion, there were two ways to divide the calendar year: (1) by the seasons or the cycles of the sun and (2) by the months or the cycles of the moon.

There were different names in different languages for the sun festivals, but the ones derived from Celtic are those used most often by witches today. Roodmas, or the May Day celebration, was a turning point in the year when planting was to begin and fertility was at its height. Lammas, on August 1, was a midsummer festival devoted to thanksgiving for a good growing season and also dedicated to the first harvest of the year. Hallowmas (or Samhain), October 31, was the most solemn of the four witch festivals, since it was a night of tribute to departed spirits and also a recognition that, like the deceased ancestors who were honored, the agricultural year was giving way to the death grip of winter. And finally, there was Candlemas, February 2, a late winter ritual during which bonfires were kindled as a harbinger of the coming fires of the sun that would again permit the planting and regeneration of the crops.

In addition to these four major festivals, witches were supposed to meet once every twenty-eight days at the full of the moon, during which time the great Earth Mother, the prototype of Mother Nature, was worshiped. Obviously, one of the major links between the moon and the human female in the ancient mind was the twenty-eight day cycle of the moon, from new moon to full moon, and the twenty-eight day menstrual cycle of a woman.

The Wicca referred to this all-powerful female deity as the "Great Horned Goddess," although they claimed that all of the fertility goddesses of ancient religions virtually amounted to the same thing. Thus goddesses such as Hecate, Diana, Artemis, and so on, became associated with the Horned Goddess. Undoubtedly, this female deity was depicted as bearing horns or a crescent shape as a crown because of the crescent shape of the moon, as well as because of the horns of the goat, long a symbol for sexual energy. It was presumably this Horned Goddess that was transmogrified into the horned devil of the Christians by Christian scholars and theologians who were convinced that the devil was behind paganism and who observed pagans celebrating the existence of a horned entity.

Lovecraft would have picked up this much information (without the references to the Wicca) from Frazer's *The Golden Bough*, and he incorporated it into his fiction. HPL makes numerous references to abominable rites being performed on May Eve and All Hallow's Eve in many of his stories, and the rituals undertaken on those nights are always directly related to the worship of his pantheon of monstrous deities.

Because Lovecraft was not overly fond of women, the strong feminine principle found in the Old Religion does not surface heavily in his tales, but it is significant that in "The Thing on the Doorstep" it is Asenath Waite, wife of Edward Pickman Derby, who seems to play the role of high priestess to her own coven of occultists, just as Wiccan covens of twelve persons are even today presided over by a thirteenth—a high priestess.

One of the excuses for the existence of the Old Religion was that its followers felt themselves empowered by the Horned Goddess to perform magical ceremonies that would ensure them a good crop yield, happiness, long life, health, and sexual prowess (which would presumably produce a large family of strong farmers, a major function of the family unit up until the Industrial Revolution). These witches would meet in desolate, untrodden settings, for secrecy's sake, and make ritual sacrifices or undertake rites using those standard witches' props, the cauldron (representing the female vessel) and the wand, broomstick, or dagger (representing the male sexual organ). If these rituals were properly executed, it was assumed that fertility would inevitably follow.

Unfortunately, however, mankind has never let its own members harmlessly pursue their own religious practices unimpeded. By the time Christianity gained a substantial foothold in western Europe, the witch cults were driven underground. To be caught in the act of practicing witchcraft was to be caught at heresy. Of course, witchcraft had been considered an evil even in pre-Christian times because it involved having commerce with the powers of darkness (literally involving the moon, the night, and secret places but symbolically involving evil spirits). But during the Middle Ages and well into the Renaissance, church theologians came to dogmatize what was believed about witchcraft, even going so far as to publish official church "position papers" about what constituted witchcraft and what did not. And as it surely had to happen, ways of discovering witches were also set down, and the famous witch hunts got under way.

It is extremely important to note here that during the height of the witchcraft madness (the sixteenth century in Europe and the seventeenth century in America), most of those accused and executed as witches were nothing of the kind. The actual number of practicing witches was probably quite small. Nevertheless, the persecutions were not entirely unjust, since many of the accused thought they *were* guilty of their supposed crime. This was because of the prevalent nature of theological belief. In those days the devil was thought of as a vital, virtually physical force in the world. Satan was believed to intervene directly in the affairs of men. Thus if a woman had an erotic dream about a man who was not her husband or if she bore a grudge against a person who suddenly died, it was a short step in the imagination to conceive of herself as possessed by unholy powers.

Since it was generally known how the devil worked and how a witch went about worshiping him, it was not difficult for a man or a woman to extend inner emotions of eroticism or hostility into the outward signs of witchcraft. Therefore, when confessions of guilt were wrung from these deluded victims, often under torture, they were on occasion confessions of perfectly normal human desires that had been translated in the victim's own mind into the acceptance of Satan as lord.

Then there were others who had consciously rejected Jesus as the true Christ and who had opted purposely for the worship of darkness.

And of course there were those few who actually were members of the Old Religion—a theological system that had nothing whatever to do with Christianity.

In any case, the witch finders of the Inquisition knew what to look for and what to do. Suspected witches who had been accused either justly or unjustly were arrested and exhorted to confess. If they did not, they were prepared for the Question. Accused witches were stripped and shaved of all their body hair (even women were often stripped and shaved publicly) in hopes of discovering a witch's mark—a mole, birthmark, or other skin irregularity that was thought to be the devil's brand. When such a mark was found, the witch was then "pricked" in that spot with a long needle; if the pricking drew no blood, it was a sure sign of witchcraft. Often, however, even a bleeding "witch's mark" would be overlooked and inhuman tortures would draw the required confessions, sometimes even from the most pious of church-goers and, not amazingly, even from accused members of the clergy.

In America the most celebrated of witchcraft occurrences was that at Salem, Massachusetts, where the inquiry into alleged cases of diabolism was occasioned by several teenaged girls who started accusing townspeople of witchcraft in jest—a jest that ended in over 200 imprisonments and 19 executions.

Lovecraft drew heavily on the witchcraft hysteria as a historical backdrop in his fiction, and particularly upon that at Salem. There were probably several reasons for this. First, to Lovecraft's scientific mind the witchcraft business was undoubtedly one of the greatest horrors imaginable, a kind of cosmic trap established and condoned by theological doctrine—the kind of trap from which there is no escape, that one has nightmares about. Second, witchcraft, as it was understood during the late Renaissance, was tailor-made for Lovecraft's fictional notions of organized cults worshiping dark powers. Only minor adjustments had to be made in the *purpose and objects* of that worship, permitting Lovecraft to explain that in fact Satan was not being idolized as was commonly thought but entities far worse than Satan, worse, as we have said, because they had actual, physical existence. And third, since Lovecraft was passionately in love with New England, the Salem witch hysteria was a genuine horrific New England event against which to set his twentieth-century New England horror tales.

Although HPL's pantheon of sinister deities was almost completely the product of his own fertile imagination, there were numerous examples of such demonic hierarchies that had been worked out by various theologians and that were believed in implicitly. The famous old religious dispute about how many angels can dance on the head of a pin may sound foolish today, but from the Middle Ages through the Renaissance, angels and demons were considered to be solid and tangible enough that their numbers could be computed and their attributes described. Demonologists (who did not practice the worship of demons but who devoted lifetimes to their study) often produced lists and even illustrated tracts on these hierarchies of devils (much like the list of Lovecraft's demons earlier in this chapter). One such list, assembled in 1589 by a demonologist named Binsfield, included Lucifer (Pride), Mammon (Avarice), Asmodeus (Lechery), Satan (Anger), Beelzebub (Gluttony), Leviathan (Envy), and Belphegor (Sloth).

Other demonological tracts made this list look simple-minded. Often such lists were broken into sections, or into several hierarchies, with certain demons belonging to one order of existence or another. One catalog of this nature was worked out in the fourth century by the Pseudo-Dionysius based on the writings of the Apostle Paul. The Pseudo-Dionysius listed nine orders of supernatural beings, with three hierarchies each of three orders.

As the so-called science of demonology became more refined, the lists of demonic hierarchies became more sophisticated until the exact number of devils in the universe could be accurately computed. One such computation counted 133,306,668 demons, while another arrived at the figure of 66 princes in command of 6,660,000 devils.

However, not only were churchly theologians devoted to demonology; a number of famous occultists were given to the same enterprise. One such occultist was Arthur Edward Waite, whose *The Book of Black Magic and of Pacts* Lovecraft confessed to having read. In that volume, Waite draws upon the information contained in other well-known magical grimoires such as *The Key of Solomon, The Lemegeton, The Grimoire of Honorius, The Book of True Black Magic,* and others in constructing the demonic pantheon. The result is an enormously complex listing of various evil spirits, guardian angels, princes, lieutenants, and so on, each of whom rules or is ruled by a different planet, element, power, or attribute. In Samuel Liddel MacGregor Mathers' translation of the grimoire known as *The Sacred Magic of Abra-Melin the Mage*, there is a list of 327 demons organized into a hierarchy and commanded by Lucifer, Leviathan, Satan, and Belial. As an indication that doctrinal disputes die hard, even among occultists, it is interesting to note that Waite and Mathers were acquainted with each other's work (both were writing about 1900) and that each considered the other a humbug.

The significance of all this to the fiction of Lovecraft is that Lovecraft also invented his own demonic pantheon, and this activity was probably suggested by other such pantheons that HPL had encountered in his reading of occult literature. Furthermore, it could be no coincidence that Lovecraft's god Azathoth so closely resembles (at least in name) the demon called Astaroth in numerous demonological lists.

Generally, though, the names of Lovecraft's monsters were not immediately connected to any demons on the actual lists but were apparently named according to what sounded authentic or hideous to Lovecraft's own ear. In this way, Yog-Sothoth evolves because of the "oth" repetition in the word that was common in the names of supposedly actual spirits. Nyarlathotep derives its name from Egyptian, and although there was no such god as Nyarlathotep in the ancient Egyptian hierarchy, the word has a convincing quality that makes us suspect that there might have been. Sadly, one cannot help but feel that the god Shub-Niggurath obtains its name as a result of Lovecraft's blanket lack of fondness for the black race. HPL owned a black cat that he named Nigger-Man, and the unpleasant epithet seems to have found its way into Shub-Niggurath's name as well. But also, we should note here the familiar "ath" suffix and the decidedly repellent-sounding "Shub" prefix. Once again, sound seems to have played the important role in the name-giving process.

THE GRIMOIRES

To give his monstrous hierarchy more credibility Lovecraft realized that being able to cite the magical text in which the demons are mentioned would be of great value. In doing his research on occult matters, Lovecraft observed that central to any system of ceremonial occultism was a grimoire, a volume that amounted to a handbook for sorcerers, containing information about infernal spirits, rituals for summoning them, how they could be ordered to depart and how the magical operator could gain from the spirits whatever it was that he wanted.

From ancient times to the present, grimoires of one kind or another have been produced. Often, a grimoire would simply show up one day in the hands of a magician with no explanation as to where it came from. Most commonly, these new grimoires had been based on much older ones, the older information having been combined with rituals invented by the magician. Sometimes, grimoires were frankly admitted to be ancient and were presented by certain occultists in English translations (an example of this is *The Sacred Magic of Abra-Melin the Mage* translated by Mathers).

Normally, books dealing with ritual magic were not nearly as old as they were reputed to be. The *Abra-Melin*, for example, was supposed to have been written by "Abraham the Jew," suggesting the biblical Abraham, but the book was probably no older than the fourteenth or fifteenth century. Nevertheless, it is possible that the rituals contained in some of the more famous grimoires date back to pre-Christian times, and in some cases (like *The Egyptian Book of the Dead*) this is absolutely certain. Among the best-known magical grimoires are the following:

1. *The Key of Solomon* was and is by far the most famous of all the grimoires, and upon studying other such books one will find elements of *The Key of Solomon* included. A book of rituals attributed to Solomon was mentioned as early as the first century *A.D.*, although the oldest known copy of *The Key* is a Greek version, possibly dating from the twelfth or thirteenth century. This copy is now in the British Museum. The influence of *The Key of Solomon* was strong enough that it was banned by the Inquisition in 1559 as fearfully dangerous.

2. *The Lesser Key of Solomon* (or the *Lemegeton*) was also attributed to Solomon and is reproduced in a slightly altered form in Waite's *The Book of Ceremonial Magic*.

3. *The Grimoire of Honorius* was first published at Rome in 1670, but it may date from the sixteenth century.

4. *The Grimorium Verum* was said to have been written in French, published in 1517, in Memphis by Alibeck the Egyptian and is based on *The Key of Solomon*.

5. *The Grand Grimoire*, written in French, probably dates from the eighteenth century.

6. *The Black Pullet*, again supposed to have been published in Egypt about 1740, nevertheless probably dates from the late eighteenth century.

These grimoires, and others like them, almost always went through editions in various languages and were written by unknown authors. They were universally suppressed by the church during the Middle Ages and the early Renaissance.

The grimoire that Lovecraft invented as a necessary coefficient to his demonic pantheon was called the *Necronomicon* and was purportedly composed by Abdul Alhazred, a mad Arab poet living at Sanaa in Yemen, in about 735 *A.D.* The *Necronomicon*'s obviously Greek title indicates a translation from the Arabic, in which language the book's original title was *Al Azif*.

Actually, throughout the Mythos stories Lovecraft is careful to drop the names of several other fictional grimoires, among them *De Vermis Mysteriis*, the *Cultes des Goules*, the *Livre d'Eibon*, and *The Pnakotic Manuscripts*. But the *Necronomicon* became the staple grimoire, as it were, and appears most regularly throughout Lovecraft's fiction. In fact, the *Necronomicon* was so real to Lovecraft that he sat down and wrote a history and publication chronology for it (see Appendix 2).

"The History and Chronology of the *Necronomicon*" is a particularly significant work for two reasons. First, after studying both Lovecraft's essay on his own grimoire and the preceding list of actual, historical incantation books, it will become clear that Lovecraft modeled the *Necronomicon* on the real thing. Consider these points of comparison:

1. The *Necronomicon* was composed by an Arab, Abdul Alhazred, just as *The Grimorum Verum* was supposed to have been published by Alibeck the Egyptian.

2. Both the *Necronomicon* and the real grimoires went through numerous translations, including Latin and various vulgate editions.

3. Both the *Necronomicon* and *The Key of Solomon* were suppressed by the church as dangerous books.

4. The British Museum now owns a Greek copy of *The Key of Solomon* just as a fifteenth-century Latin text of the *Necronomicon* is owned by the British Museum.

But there was a second consequence of Lovecraft's "History and Chronology of the *Necronomicon*," one that was fairly bizarre by any standard. Apparently, Lovecraft had done such a convincing job of making his grimoire sound authentic (even down to listing the university libraries where copies could be secured) that some of HPL's readers started out in search of the book. For a time, librarians and bookstore owners were annoyed by people trying to buy or borrow the *Necronomicon*. For all anybody knows, this may still be going on.

Yet it is a fact that a New York bookseller listed a copy of the *Necronomicon* in his catalog for $375, an edition that apparently no one was successful in purchasing. And it is also a fact that the John Hay Library at Providence, Rhode Island's Brown University does indeed hold a copy of *Al Azif* by Abdul Alhazred, written in Duraic and published by the Owl's Wick Press of Philadelphia in 1973. It seems that where Lovecraft is concerned, truth and fiction are merely relative.

MONSTERS ETERNAL

As always in Lovecraft, a solid basis in historical fact is one of the most powerful elements in the fiction. The HPL Mythos tales modify occult historical fact in an attempt to suggest that the Mythos gods might be at the root of it all, and in fact this is explicitly stated, particularly in stories like "The Dreams in the Witch-House," "The Call of Cthulhu," and "The Case of Charles Dexter Ward." In effect, the Mythos monsters resonate throughout Lovecraft's stories, whether they actually appear onstage at any given moment or not. Somehow, we always know that Yog-Sothoth and Azathoth are with us. This is true not only because the monsters pervade the tales but also because occult history pervades the tales. The result of this is that through an illogical and emotional form of transitive property we come to connect HPL's monsters with real events and real occult beliefs. And if others have believed in these creatures, or some version of them, over the centuries, our belief in them is suddenly much more sensible and better founded than if we were reading a conventional horror story.

And here we come to what separates Lovecraft from other writers of weird fiction. Whereas many authors might present us with a papier-maché ghost or an enraged elf, giving us a scare that lasts about a half-hour, Lovecraft surrounds us with cosmic demons whose existence is supported by history and whose appearances in specific places at specific times have been chronicled. And, above all, they are monsters that do not perish at the end of the story and were not born at the beginning of the story. HPL's creations are things, in a way, that have become quite distinct from their creator, much as Sherlock Holmes stepped out of Sir Arthur Conan Doyle's mind and continues to live in Baker Street forty years after the death of his creator.

Of course, Lovecraft's monsters share with Holmes a kind of universality. We want to believe in Holmes because he is the paradigm of justice and good. Similarly, we must also want to believe in Lovecraft's monsters because, subconsciously, we are aware that for good to exist there must be evil. Lovecraft's grisly crew is virtually the model for evil, and this is so for two reasons. First, the Mythos pantheon itself is representative of universal evil simply because the influence of those deities stretches across the entire cosmos. And, second, Lovecraft makes it clear that the notion of universal evil and its oddly attractive power appeal to human beings because there is never a shortage of those ready and willing to sink down on their knees and worship it.

So Lovecraft is really playing on the dual nature of the reader. On the one hand, he is aligning the reader with the forces of good that constantly try to erase the monsters from the universe. But, at the same time, he also seems aware that we are subconsciously cheering the monsters on. We are "pulling for" the monsters merely by dint of the fact that we believe they exist. And it is belief that permits the existence of what we cannot scientifically prove to exist, not the other way around as Dr. Van Helsing would have us think in *Dracula*. The result of all this is fear coupled with fascination, the variety of frightened fascination one feels when he thinks he sees a ghost but simply cannot look away from the horrifying yet awe-inspiring sight.

Lovecraft has achieved a literary reality that few other authors in history have been able to emulate. Seldom in all of literature has any writer invented fictional cities that readers have tried to find on roadmaps, a university that has been hunted for in registers of colleges, a fictional book that was almost sold to several serious book collectors, and a mythology of gods that seems to have been lifted directly from a medieval tract on demonology.

In fact, Lovecraft's Mythos has come to be so pervasive among those interested in the occult today that at least one practicing ceremonial magician has incorporated it into his book of rituals. Anton Szandor LaVey, presently the head of the Church of Satan, published his *The Satanic Rituals* in 1972. LaVey is a self-styled magician and is considered by many occultists to be a fraud and a charlatan. Nevertheless, to his hundreds of followers he is the real thing; and even those who dislike him must admit that he has more than a modicum of ritual knowledge.

Chapter Eight of *The Satanic Rituals* is entirely devoted to "The Metaphysics of Lovecraft" and includes "The Ceremony of the Nine Angles" and "The Call to Cthulhu." These rituals are of LaVey's own invention (a standard practice among ceremonial magicians, who are presumably following their own genius in the construction of new rituals) and rely heavily on the snatches of the *Necronomicon* that we get in the stories as well as other fictional elements of Lovecraft's creation. LaVey even went so far as to make up long passages in the language of the *Necronomicon* and then "translate" them back into English.

After Lovecraft's death (and even in the later years of his life) there were members of the HPL literary circle who found the Mythos a fertile enough field to support other stories. Writers such as Robert Bloch, J. Ramsay Campbell, August Derleth, Clark Ashton Smith, Robert E. Howard, Brian Lumley, and others turned out Mythos stories of their own. Normally, these tales were not as good as Lovecraft's own, but they did and still continue to indicate the grip of the Mythos on the popular imagination.

But Lovecraftian Mythos pastiches were not to be confined only to the genre of weird fiction. In 1968 Harcourt, Brace and World, Incorporated, published a Lovecraft pastiche that is unknown even to most HPL devotees. *Dagon* by Fred Chappell was not intended to be merely a horror story in the pulp magazine tradition but is a serious experimental novel dealing with human degradation, the problem of evil and man's weakness to resist it. The epigram for Chappell's *Dagon* is the line "Ph'nglui mglw'nafh Cthulhu R'lyeh wgah'nagl fhtagn," taken directly from "The Call of Cthulhu," and the book's antagonist is a backwoods North Carolina girl who has that strange, fishy "Innsmouth look" that HPL described in "The Shadow over Innsmouth."

These appearances of H. P. Lovecraft's cosmos in places where one would not expect to find them are a tribute to HPL's power as a writer and a creator of vistas of evil. And it is undoubtedly safe to presume that although Lovecraft himself has passed from this world, the demons he brought forth will live long after him.

The order of the golden dawn

Just before the turn of the century, there emerged in England one of the most celebrated societies dedicated to the practice of ceremonial magic ever to exist. It was called the Hermetic Order of the Golden Dawn, and it counted among its members some of the day's most illustrious men and women. Irish poet and mystic W. B. Yeats belonged, as did Aleister Crowley, the most famous magus of modern times and a man reputed by the press to be the "wickedest" on earth. Robert Louis Stevenson was said to have been tangentially associated with the Golden Dawn, and other members of note included horror story writers Algernon Blackwood and Arthur Machen as well as occultists Samuel Liddel MacGregor Mathers and Arthur Edward Waite.

The Golden Dawn is thought to have been formed about 1880 when a member of the hermetic Rosicrucians discovered some cipher documents of magical importance in either a Freemason or a Rosicrucian library. These documents were translated from their arcane language into English by Dr. William Westcott and MacGregor Mathers, the resultant text providing the basis for the Golden Dawn rituals.

The purpose of the Golden Dawn was the study and practice of ceremonial magic, and it is important to understand just what is meant by that. High ceremonial magic, like most mystical religions, certain forms of yoga, the Hebrew Kabbala, and even the refined forms of what has come to be called Transcendental Meditation, is designed to permit its practitioner to free himself from the materialistic bonds of this world and gain knowledge of the deepest secrets of existence. Operations like conjuring up demons, controlling the weather or the state of one's finances, and so on, are simply practiced in order that the practitioner may become adept at imposing his will over nature. These techniques are finally put to the test later in the magician's career when he uses them for the Great Work of revealing the Truth of the Universe.

The Golden Dawn rituals that derived from the Rosicrucian documents, plus others added later by Golden Dawn members, drew upon a vast range of mystical and religious tradition. Hebrew Kabbalism played a very important role as did elements of Babylonian, Greek, Egyptian, Hindu, and Buddhist mythology. There were also certain strong influences of Christian mysticism.

The society was organized into ten grades or levels of magical attainment, beginning with the Neophyte and progressing upward to the Ipsissimus, whose knowledge surpassed human understanding. Presiding over the Golden Dawn was a Grand Master who was directly responsible to the Secret Chiefs, although it is unclear whether this latter title represented human or superhuman agencies.

Aleister Crowley, already learned in occult science, joined the Golden Dawn in 1898 and quickly rose to prominence within the order. As his influence grew, a power struggle arose between Crowley and MacGregor Mathers, eventually causing a schism in the membership. Crowley became Grand Master of the order, and Mathers took his faction to Paris, where he set up his own temple. It was during this period that two events of importance occurred: (1) a magical war between Crowley and Mathers and (2) Crowley's publication of the Golden Dawn's secret rituals.

Because of the hatred that existed between Crowley and Mathers, the latter (according to Crowley) began to send magical forces against his enemy. Crowley awoke one morning to find his bedroom full of strange, horned beetles, which he repelled through the exercise of his own magic. As things finally developed, it was not Crowley who had to take the final steps against Mathers. Crowley's version of the story is that Mathers destroyed himself through performing a magical ritual that he was not prepared to undertake.

One of Mathers' greatest accomplishments as a magician-scholar was his translation of a reputedly ancient Hebrew grimoire called *The Sacred Magic of Abra-Melin the Mage*. This book is a unified magical system whose preparations and rituals take about a year to complete. After Mathers translated it, he tried it out. But, supposedly, Mathers was already in disfavor with the Secret Chiefs, and this, along with his lack of spiritual readiness, not only prevented him from successfully gaining magical knowledge from the Abra-Melin operation but also caused him to fall into dissolution. He turned to drink, began forcing his wife to model in the nude for Paris artists, and eventually lost his effectiveness as a magical leader.

A little after the turn of the century, Crowley, feeling that he was acting on orders from the Secret Chiefs, began publishing the hitherto closely guarded rituals of the order. It was Crowley's intention to start a magical millennium, but the publications only enraged other members of the Golden Dawn. Yet Crowley's power and "powers" were apparently strong enough so that he encountered little resistance.

Crowley brought out the Golden Dawn documents in ten beautifully bound and printed magazines called *The Equinox*, which began publication in the first decade of the century, was interrupted by World War I, and resumed for a short time thereafter. By 1937, since the documents had been released anyway (albeit in Crowley's veiled, metaphorical rhetoric that was almost impossible to understand), another Golden Dawn member named Israel Regardie undertook a massive four-volume simplification of the rituals. This book, *The Golden Dawn*, naturally angered Crowley, probably because it was so much more lucid than his *Equinox*.

These books, *The Equinox* and *The Golden Dawn*, are important to a study of H. P Lovecraft for several reasons. First, they are the closest thing to Lovecraft's *Necronomicon* to be produced in this century. Second, in his study of occult material, it is not impossible that Lovecraft may have come into contact with *The Equinox*. In fact, the Widener Library at Harvard owns Volume I, Number 5 (March 1911), of *The Equinox*, which was received at the library on December 31, 1917, placing it easily within Lovecraft's reach. And third, there is a kind of peripheral connection between Lovecraft and the Golden Dawn in that several of his favorite weird fiction writers belonged to it. Arthur Machen and Algernon Blackwood, both of whom Lovecraft praised (albeit to different degrees) in "Supernatural Horror in Literature," were prominent members of the order, as were Sax Rohmer, Bram Stoker, author of *Dracula*, and Robert Louis Stevenson.

Another Golden Dawn initiate to whom Lovecraft seems obliquely to refer in his fiction was the highly respected Kabbalist, Arthur Edward Waite. Lovecraft seems to have had Waite's surname stuck in his mind, since he uses it in three separate stories, "The Case of Charles Dexter Ward," "The Shadow over Innsmouth," and notably in "The Thing on the Doorstep," in which it is the scion of "the Innsmouth Waites" who is the villain. "The Thing on the Doorstep" begins with the marriage of Edward Pickman Derby, a student of the occult who is familiar with the *Necronomicon*, to a woman named Asenath Waite, daughter of the magician Ephriam Waite. Combining Edward Derby with Asenath Waite brings us, whether Lovecraft consciously intended it or whether it was a subconscious memory, to Arthur *Edward Waite.*

This theory really is not as bizarre as it sounds. Waite, an occultist who died in 1942, was and still is well known in both Europe and America. In 1898 he published *The Book of Black Magic and of Pacts*, which became quite popular owing to its rather sensationalistic title. Because the book was not protected by any international copyright laws at the time it was published, a number of American houses began to issue pirated editions in the United States—fourteen in all. Later, Waite reorganized the book and had it copyrighted under the title *The Book of Ceremonial Magic: A Complete Grimoire.* It was very probably from *The Book of Black Magic and of Pacts* that Lovecraft derived much of his information on *The Keys of Solomon*, the grimoire mentioned in "Supernatural Horror in Literature," and which is reprinted in Waite. Waite was also the author of a voluminous amount of material on the Hebrew holy Kabbala.

Kabbalism is a branch of magical study dealing with interpretations of existence that are veiled by certain numerological and linguistic features of the Hebrew language. This is why it was prerequisite for all Golden Dawn initiates to learn Hebrew. An interesting facet of this study is the practice of interpreting the letters of a word as representative of a whole sentence. This part of Kabbalism is referred to as *Notarikon*, and suggests both the cryptic rhetorical form and the name of Lovecraft's *Necronomicon*.

This is not to say that the rituals of the *Necronomicon* and of the Golden Dawn documents have very much in common. The Great Work of Golden Dawn initiates was to raise their level of consciousness to a point at which the scheme and design of universal existence would be revealed. The various forms of magical study and the hermetric ritual operations were all, in one way or another, intended to contribute to this end.

The rituals of the *Necronomicon*, on the other hand, are purely a means by which to liberate the demonic Old Ones from their trans-dimensional domain or terrestrial slumber. The *Necronomicon* is referred to by Lovecraft as an "accursed" book precisely because it contains information that would madden even an extraordinarily strong-minded man and because it spells out magical incantations that hold the potential of man's extermination by the Old Ones.

Yet the similarities between the Golden Dawn and the cult of the *Necronomicon*, as well as the connection between the members of the British mystical society and horror fiction, must surely strike the reader of Lovecraft as remarkable.

"The history and chronology of the *Necronomicon*" by H. P. Lovecraft

Original title *Al Azif — Azif* being the word used by the Arabs to designate that nocturnal sound (made by insects) supposed to be the howling of demons.

Composed by Abdul Alhazred, a mad poet of Sanaa, in Yemen, who is said to have flourished during the period of the Ommiade Caliphs, circa *A.D.* 700. He visited the ruins of Babylon and the subterranean secrets of Memphis and spent ten years alone in the great southern desert of Arabia — the Roba el Ehaliyeh or "Empty Space" of the ancients and "Dahna" or "Crimson Desert" of the modern Arabs, which is held to be inhabited by protective evil spirits and monsters of death. Of this desert many strange and unbelievable marvels are told by those who pretend to have penetrated it. In his last years Alhazred dwelt in Damascus, where the *Necronomicon* (*Al Azif*) was written, and of his final death or disappearance (*A.D.* 738) many terrible and conflicting things are told. He is said by Ebn Khallikan (twelfth-century biographer) to have been seized by an invisible monster in broad daylight and devoured horribly before a large number of fright-frozen witnesses. Of his madness many things are told. He claimed to have seen the fabulous Irem, or City of Pillars, and to have found beneath the ruins of a certain nameless desert town the shocking annals and secrets of a race older than mankind. . . . He was only an indifferent Moslem, worshipping unknown Entities whom he called Yog-Sothoth and Cthulhu.

In *A.D.* 950 the *Azif*, which had gained a considerable though surreptitious circulation amongst the philosophers of the age, was secretly translated into Greek by Theodorus Philetas of Constantinople under the title *Necronomicon*. For a century it impelled certain experimenters to terrible attempts, when it was suppressed and burnt by the patriarch Michael. After this it was only heard of furtively, but (1228) Olaus Wormius made a Latin translation later in the Middle Ages, and the Latin text was printed twice—once in the fifteenth century in black letter (evidently in Germany) and once in the seventeenth (probably Spanish); both editions being without identifying marks, and located as to time and place by internal typographical evidence only. The work, both Latin and Greek, was banned by Pope Gregory IX in 1232 shortly after its Latin translation, which called attention to it. The Arabic original was lost in Wormius' time, as indicated by his prefatory note; (there is, however, a vague account of a secret copy appearing in San Francisco during the present century but later perishing by fire) and no sight of the Greek copy—which was printed in Italy between 1500 and 1550—has been reported since the burning of a certain Salem man's library in 1692. A translation made by Dr. Dee was never printed, and exists only in fragments recovered from the original manuscript. Of the Latin texts now existing one (fifteenth century) is known to be in the British Museum under lock and key, while another (seventeenth century) is in the Bibliothèque Nationale at Paris. A seventeenth century edition is in the Widener Library at Harvard, and in the library at Miskatonic University at Arkham; also in the library of the University of Buenos Aires. Numerous other copies probably exist in secret, and a fifteenth century one is persistently rumored to form part of the collection of a celebrated American millionaire. A still vaguer rumor credits the preservation of a sixteenth century Greek text in the Salem family of Pickman, but if it was so preserved, it vanished with the artist R. U. Pickman, who disappeared in 1926. The book is rigidly suppressed by the authorities of most countries, and by all branches of organized ecclesiasticism. Reading leads to horrible consequences. It was from rumors of this book (of which relatively few of the general public know) that R. W. Chambers is said to have derived the idea of his early novel *The King in Yellow*.

1. *Al Azif* written circa *A.D.* 730 at Damascus by Abdul Alhazred.

2. Translated into Greek as *Necronomicon*, *A.D.* 950 by Theodorus Philetas.
3. Burnt by Patriarch Michael *A.D.* 1050 (i.e., Greek text) . . . (Arabic text now lost).
4. Olaus translates Greek to Latin, *A.D.* 1228.
5. Latin and Greek editions suppressed by Gregory IX— *A.D.* 1232.
6. Black letter edition. Germany—1400?
7. Greek text printed in Italy—1500-1550
8. Spanish translation of Latin text—1600?

[*Note:* Since the publication in 1938 of H. P. Lovecraft's essay on the *Necronomicon*, at least one more copy of this obviously rare book has surfaced and is now in the collection of the library at Brown University, Providence, Rhode Island. Printed by the Owl's Wick Press at Philadelphia in 1973, this modern edition of the *Necronomicon* appears to be a facsimile of the original Arabic text that Lovecraft presumed lost by the year *A.D.* 1050. A problematical aspect of the Brown University copy, however, is that the text, though appearing to the untrained eye to be in Arabic, is actually in a language known to Semitic scholars as Duraic. Unfortunately, there has, to date, been no successful completion of a translation. —P.A.S.]

Selected bibliography

The difficulties of compiling a comprehensive H. P. Lovecraft bibliography are many, primarily because much of Lovecraft's work was originally published in small-print-run limited editions or in what we now refer to as "little magazines" of amateur journalist associations and science fiction fan groups. In addition, his work has also appeared in over 150 anthologies of various kinds. Much of this material, together with the greatest number of critical studies on Lovecraft, is to be found in the collections of the John Hay Library at Providence, Rhode Island's Brown University and in the New York City Public Library, as well as in several extensive private collections around the country.

From the year 1939 to the present Arkham House Publishers of Sauk City, Wisconsin, have brought out the widest variety of Lovecraft fiction, poetry, essays, and criticism. However, Arkham House print runs tend to be small, and many of these editions are now out of print. Only since about 1970 has Lovecraft's work been made available to the general reader in inexpensive soft-bound editions.

Therefore, this bibliography is not meant to be inclusive. Its purpose is to provide the reader with a functional listing of books by, about, and related to Lovecraft. If certain editions are out of print, that fact will be noted.

I. Lovecraft Collections

Lovecraft, H. P. *At the Mountains of Madness and Other Novels*. Sauk City, Wis.: Arkham House, 1964. A collection of Lovecraft's longer fiction works.

———. *At the Mountains of Madness*. New York: Ballantine, 1973. A soft-cover edition containing three longer works and a short story.

———. *Beyond the Wall of Sleep*. Sauk City, Wis.: Arkham House, 1943. Contains fiction by Lovecraft, plus Lovecraft-style fiction and criticism by other hands. Out of print.

———. *The Case of Charles Dexter Ward*. New York: Ballantine, 1971. Lovecraft's short novel of necromancy and magic reaching across the centuries.

———. *The Colour Out of Space*. New York: Lancer Books, 1964. A soft-cover book containing eight of Lovecraft's best stories. Out of print.

———. *The Colour Out of Space*. New York: Zebra Books, 1975. A soft-cover reprint of the Lancer edition.

———. *Dagon and Other Macabre Tales*. Sauk City, Wis.: Arkham House, 1965. Contains much of Lovecraft's early fiction, plus his essay "Supernatural Horror in Literature."

———. *The Dark Brotherhood and Other Pieces*. Sauk City, Wis.: Arkham House, 1966. Contains essays by Lovecraft and fiction and criticism from other hands. Out of print.

———. *The Doom That Came to Sarnath*. New York: Ballantine, 1971. A paperback reprint of much of Lovecraft's early work, including a number of prose fragments.

———. *The Dream-Quest of Unknown Kadath*. New York: Ballantine, 1970. Contains six of Lovecraft's dreamland stories.

———. *The Dunwich Horror and Others*. Sauk City, Wis.: Arkham House, 1966. Contains fifteen of Lovecraft's best mature fictional works.

———. *The Dunwich Horror*. New York: Lancer Books, 1963. Contains six of the fifteen stories from the Arkham House edition. Out of print.

———. *The Horror in the Museum and Other Revisions*. Sauk City, Wis.: Arkham House, 1970. Contains stories ghost-written by Lovecraft for other writers.

———. *The Horror in the Museum and Other Revisions*. New York: Ballantine, 1971. Softbound reprint of the Arkham House edition.

———. *The Lurking Fear and Other Tales*. New York: Ballantine, 1973. A good mixture of early and mature Lovecraft fiction.

———. *Marginalia*. Sauk City, Wis.: Arkham House, 1944. A collection of Lovecraft's fiction and essays together with criticism from other hands. Out of print.

———. *The Outsider and Others*. Sauk City, Wis.: Arkham House, 1939. The first Lovecraft collection, featuring thirty-seven works of fiction plus "Supernatural horror in Literature." Out of print.

———. *Something About Cats and Other Pieces*. Sauk City, Wis.: Arkham House, 1949. Essays and poetry by Lovecraft, essays and fiction from other hands. Out of print.

———. *Something About Cats and Other Pieces*. Plainview, N.Y.: Books for Libraries, 1971. A cloth-bound reprint of the Arkham House edition.

———. *Supernatural Horror in Literature*. New York: Dover Publications, 1975. A new, softbound edition of Lovecraft's classic essay.

———. *The Tomb and Other Tales*. New York: Ballantine, 1973. A sampling of Lovecraft's early and mature fiction, plus some prose fragments.

II. Pastiches

Both during Lovecraft's life and after his death a number of other writers became magnetically attracted to the Mythos cycle and produced tales using the settings and monsters Lovecraft created. New Mythos tales and novels are being produced even now—so rapidly that bibliographers are hard-pressed to keep up with them. A good place to start, however, in becoming acquainted with the HPL pastiche writers is the following set of books:

Carter, Lin, ed. *The Spawn of Cthulhu*. New York: Ballantine, 1971. A collection of Mythos stories by Lovecraft and others, including earlier stories that influenced and informed the Mythos.

Derleth, August. *The Mask of Cthulhu*. London: Neville Spearman, 1974. A collection of Derleth's own pastiches of HPL.

———. *The Mask of Cthulhu*. New York: Ballantine, 1971. Softbound reprint of the Spearman edition.

———, ed. *Tales of the Cthulhu Mythos, Volume I*. New York: Ballantine, 1973. Contains Mythos stories by Lovecraft and members of his circle.

— — —, ed. *Tales of Cthulhu Mythos, Volume II*. New York: Ballantine, 1973. More Mythos stories by Lovecraft, his circle, and some younger writers.

— — —. *The Trail of Cthulhu*. London: Neville Spearman, 1974. A second volume of pastiches by Derleth alone.

— — —. *The Trail of Cthulhu*. New York: Ballantine, 1971. Softbound reprint of the Spearman edition.

Lovecraft, H. P., and August Derleth. *The Lurker at the Threshold*. New York: Ballantine, 1971. A collection of the so-called Lovecraft-Derleth posthumous collaborations in which Derleth wrote Mythos stories based on rough notes or outlines left by Lovecraft after his death.

— — —. *The Shuttered Room and Other Tales*. New York: Ballantine, 1973. More Lovecraft-Derleth Mythos collaborations.

— — —. *The Survivor and Others*. New York: Ballantine, 1962. Still more Lovecraft-Derleth collaborations.

— — —. *The Watchers Out of Time*. Sauk City, Wis.: Arkham House, 1974. A collection of all the Lovecraft-Derleth posthumous collaborations.

Lumley, Brian. *Beneath the Moors*. Sauk City, Wis.: Arkham House, 1974. This young British writer uses the Yorkshire moors as a setting for a Mythos story of a subterranean city and the things that built it.

— — —. *The Burrowers Beneath*. New York: DAW Books, 1974. Lumley introduces Titus Crow in a tale of "the world's real landlords."

— — —. *The Caller of the Black*. Sauk City, Wis.: Arkham House, 1971. A collection of Mythos-related short stories.

— — —. *The Transition of Titus Crow*. New York: DAW Books, 1975. A space-time adventure involving the Elder Gods.

Wilson, Colin. *The Mind Parasites*. Berkeley, Calif.: Oneiric Press, 1967. In this, as in Wilson's other two Lovecraft-related books, the prominent social philosopher uses the Mythos to investigate his theories of "evolutionary existentialism."

— — —. *The Outsider*. Boston: Houghton Mifflin, 1956.

— — —. *The Philosopher's Stone*. New York: Warner Paperback Library, 1974.

III. Lovecraft Biographies

Carter, Lin. *Lovecraft: A Look Behind the Cthulhu Mythos*. New York: Ballantine, 1972. A good general literary biography of Lovecraft, containing bibliography, but no notes or index.

Conover, Willis. *Lovecraft at Last*. Arlington, Va.: Carrollton Clark, 1975. A reminiscence of the last months of Lovecraft's life. A beautiful, if expensive, book replete with photographs, manuscript reproductions, etc.

De Camp, L. Sprague. *Lovecraft: A Biography*. Garden City, N.Y.: Doubleday and Company, 1975. An exhaustive, major biography of HPL, the best to date, with notes, bibliography, and index and a wealth of information about Lovecraft's life and works.

— — —. *Lovecraft: A Biography*. New York: Ballantine, 1976. A paperback abridgement of the hardcover biography, minus the notes, bibliography, index, and a number of photos.

Derleth, August. *HPL: A Memoir*. New York: Ben Abramson, Publisher, 1945. Derleth's personal reminiscences, plus a critical evaluation of HPL's work. Out of print.

Long, Frank Belknap. *H. P. Lovecraft: Dreamer on the Night Side.* Sauk City, Wis.: Arkham House, 1975. Another personal reminiscence by a member of the Lovecraft Circle and a close friend of HPL.

IV. Bibliographies

Owings, Mark, and Irving Binkin. *A Catalogue of Lovecraftiana*. Baltimore: Mirage Press, 1975. A catalog of the holdings in the Grill-Binkin Collection, one of the largest private collections of Lovecraftiana.

Owings, Mark, and Jack Chalker. *The Revised H. P. Lovecraft Bibliography*. Baltimore: Mirage Press, 1973. One of the most useful HPL bibliographies now in print, although it contains some technical errors and omissions of more recent Lovecraft material.

Weinberg, R. E, and E. P. Berglund. *A Reader's Guide to the Cthulhu Mythos*. Albuquerque, N.M.: Silver Scarab Press, 1973. A complete bibliography of Mythos stories by Lovecraft and others, as well as of much fiction that is only remotely concerned with the Mythos.

V. Periodicals Related to Lovecraft

This section indexes some of the major periodicals concerning H. P. Lovecraft. In addition to several large-circulation magazines, numerous little magazines devoted to science fiction and fantasy are listed. Known as "fanzines" among devotees of fantasy and S-F, there are literally hundreds of these limited-circulation periodicals that touch on

Lovecraft at least once in a while. To list them all would be virtually impossible. Only those among the most important are indexed here.

The Arkham Collector. Sauk City, Wis.: Arkham House. A quarterly publication consisting of ten issues from Summer 1967 to Summer 1971. Containing fiction, poetry, and critical essays related to Lovecraft. Meant to be the successor to *The Arkham Sampler*.

The Arkham Sampler. Sauk City, Wis.: Arkham House. A quarterly publication consisting of eight issues from Spring 1948 to Winter 1949. Containing fiction, poetry, and essays related to Lovecraft and science fiction in general. Contains the first publication of "The Dream-Quest of Unknown Kadath," plus works by Ray Bradbury, Clark Ashton Smith, August Derleth, and others.

Fantasy and Terror. P.O. Box 89517, Zenith, Washington, 98188. A fantastic fiction magazine, currently being published, sometimes containing new Mythos stories.

HPL. P.O. Box 9032, Crestline Heights, Birmingham, Alabama, 35213. Not properly a magazine but really a book in magazine format containing fiction, poetry, and essays on Lovecraftian subjects. Out of print.

Journal of the H. P. Lovecraft Society. 1315 Monterey Street, Richmond, California, 94804. At this writing, only two issues of this new magazine, which appears irregularly, have been published. Contains articles by Fritz Leiber.

L'Herne. No. 12, Paris: Diffusion Minard, 1969. A special issue of the famous French literary magazine devoted completely to fiction and essays by and about Lovecraft. In French.

Nyctalops. 500 Wellesley, S.E., Albuquerque, New Mexico, 87106. A little magazine devoted to fiction, poetry, and essays often touching on Lovecraft.

Science-Fantasy Correspondent. 9122 Rosslyn, Arlington, Virginia, 22209. Currently being published, this is the recrudescence of a little magazine first published in 1936. Its contents are almost wholly Lovecraft oriented.

Weirdbook. Box 35, Amherst Branch, Buffalo, New York, 14226. A little magazine of weird fiction and poetry, often Lovecraftian.

Weird Tales. Chicago and New York: Popular Fiction Publishing Company. Published between 1923 and 1954, *Weird Tales* was the premier fantasy and horror magazine. Many of its issues contain fiction and other work by Lovecraft and members of his circle. In addition, Lovecraft is often mentioned in the letters department of many, many issues.

Whispers. 5508 Dodge Drive, Fayetteville, North Carolina, 28303. Called by many the true heir to the mantle of *Weird Tales*, this magazine currently publishes only the best fantastic fiction, much of it related to Lovecraft and his Mythos.

Witchcraft and Sorcery. 1855 West Main Street, Alhambra, California, 91801 (editorial address: P.O. Box 1331, Atlanta, Georgia, 30301). Another little magazine devoted to the publication of weird fiction in the Lovecraft tradition.

VI. Books on the Occult Related to Lovecraft

Cavendish, Richard. *The Black Arts*. New York: G. P. Putnam's Sons, 1967. A general orientation to ritual magic and the occult.

Crowley, Aleister. *The Confessions of Aleister Crowley: An Autohagiography*, ed. John Symonds and Kenneth Grant. New York: Hill and Wang, 1969. Crowley's massive and remarkable autobiography.

— —. *Gems from the Equinox*, ed. Israel Regardie. St. Paul, Minn.: Llewellyn Publications, 1974. A reprint of most of the material published in Aleister Crowley's periodical, *The Equinox*.

— —. *Magick in Theory and Practice*. New York: Castle Books, n.d. A collection of documents by Crowley on ceremonial magic. Highly technical and not for the novice.

— —. *Moonchild*. New York: Avon Books, 1971. Crowley's novel concerning magical initiation. Quite symbolic, but worth reading.

Frazer, James George. *The Golden Bough*. New York: The Macmillan Company, 1963. The classic study of ancient fertility cults with much information on the deities, their ritual worship, and magical practice. Studied by Lovecraft.

LaVey, Anton Szandor. *The Satanic Rituals*. New York: Avon Books, 1972. Some rituals of the Church of Satan, founded by LaVey. Contains rituals based on Lovecraft's writings.

Lovecraft, H. P., and Anthony Raven. *The Occult Lovecraft*. Saddle River, N.J.: Gerry de la Ree, 1975. A pamphlet that contains much useful information by and about Lovecraft and the use of occult motifs in his fiction.

Mathers, S. L. MacGregor. *The Book of the Sacred Magic of Abra-Melin the Mage*. Chicago: De Laurence Company, 1948. The

complete Abra-Melin magical grimoire translated into English by
    Mathers.
Murray, Margaret. *The Witch-Cult in Western Europe*. Oxford:
    Clarendon Press, 1921. The standard authoritative text on the
    subject, a book Lovecraft confessed having read.
Paulsen, Kathryn. *The Complete Book of Magic and Witchcraft*. New
    York: Signet, 1970. A general book on magical practice drawn
    from numerous grimoires.
Robbins, Rossell Hope. *The Encyclopedia of Witchcraft and Demon-
    ology*. New York: Crown Publishers, Inc., 1963. An encyclopedic
    treatment of the witchcraft phenomenon in the sixteenth through
    the eighteenth centuries.
Waite, Arthur Edward. *The Book of Ceremonial Magic: A Complete
    Grimoire*. New York: Citadel Press, 1970. Waite's composite
    grimoire drawn largely from the *Key of Solomon*. Lovecraft knew
    this under its earlier title, *The Book of Black Magic and of Pacts*.

VII. Historical Works Related to Lovecraft

Bonfanti, Leo. *The Witchcraft Hysteria of 1692*. Wakefield, Mass.:
    1971. A pamphlet giving a good general account of the Salem,
    Massachusetts, witchcraft horrors.
Drake, Samuel Adams. *A Book of New England Legends and Folk
    Lore*. Rutland, Vt.: Charles E. Tuttle Company, 1971. This is a
    photostatic reprint of the original 1884 edition of Adams's book.
    It contains a wealth of New England folklore, some of which was
    incorporated by Lovecraft into his fiction.
Gamage, Virginia C., and Priscilla Lord. *The Lure of Marblehead*.
    Marblehead, Mass.: Marblehead Publications, 1973. A fine pam-
    phlet history of Marblehead (Lovecraft's Kingsport), with photo-
    graphs, illustrations, and maps.
Hansen, Chadwick. *Witchcraft at Salem*. New York: Mentor Books,
    1969. One of the most spirited accounts of witchcraft in Salem,
    arguing that witchcraft was actually being practiced in New Eng-
    land in the seventeenth century.
Phillips, James Duncan. *Salem in the Seventeenth Century*. Boston:
    Houghton Mifflin Company, 1933.
– – –. *Salem in the Eighteenth Century*. Salem, Mass.: The Essex
    Institute, 1969. Together, these two books are remarkably com-
    plete histories of Salem (Lovecraft's Arkham).

Starkey, Marion L. *The Devil in Massachusetts: A Modern Enquiry into the Salem Witch Trials*. New York: Anchor Books, 1969.

Stevens, Austin N., ed. *Mysterious New England*. Dublin, N.H.: Yankee Inc., 1971. An anthology of bizarre New England occurrences and folk tales assembled by the staff of *Yankee* magazine.

VIII. Societies Devoted to Lovecraft

The Esoteric Order of Dagon. This is an active amateur press association devoted to publishing small, limited-edition periodicals related to HPL. Membership in the order is limited to thirty-nine, but there is a waiting list for those occasions when openings occur. Members of the order are responsible for publishing their own little magazines of hitherto unprinted fact and fiction about Lovecraft. Lapses in membership occur when members do not produce the requisite number of periodical pages per year.

The H. P. Lovecraft Society. This society was formed in California in 1975 and centers on science fiction and fantasy writer Fritz Leiber. Lifetime membership is $5.00, and membership cards are signed by Leiber. The society publishes *The Journal of the H. P. Lovecraft Society* at $2.50 for a single issue or $10.00 for a five-issue subscription (1315 Monterey Street, Richmond, California, 94804).

Index

About the Author

Philip A. Shreffler, an assistant professor of English at St. Louis Community College at Meramec, specializes in nineteenth-century American literature, horror fiction, and attendant folklore. A book critic for *The St. Louis Post-Dispatch* and a member of the Baker Street Irregulars of New York, he has written articles for such journals as *The Baker Street Journal, The Connecticut Critic,* and *Galaxy*.